Capitalizing on Dreams: Guide to U.S. IPO & Listings

[This Page is Intentionally Left Blank]

Capitalizing on Dreams: Guide to U.S. IPO & Listings

IPO DreamWorks Series - *"Capitalizing on Dreams: a Comprehensive Guide to U.S. IPO & Listings* • *The Road to Riches - from Garage to NASDAQ & NYSE* • *The Playbook for Going Public in America"*

Copyright © 2024 by Sean Jiang (the Author), US International Finance Foundation & United Securities Legal Group (the Publishers).

All rights reserved. No part of this publication may be reproduced, distributed or transmitted in any form or by any means, including photocopying, recording, or other electronic or mechanical methods, without the prior written permission of the author and the publisher, except in the case of brief quotations embodied in critical reviews and certain other noncommercial uses permitted by copyright law.

Although the author and publisher have made every effort to ensure that the information in this book was correct at press time, the author and publisher do not assume and hereby disclaim any liability to any party for any loss, damage, or disruption caused by errors or omissions, whether such errors or omissions result from negligence, accident, or any other cause.

Adherence to all applicable laws and regulations, including international, federal, state and local governing professional licensing, business practices, advertising, and all other aspects of doing business in the US, Canada or any other jurisdictions is the sole responsibility of the reader and consumer.

Capitalizing on Dreams: Guide to U.S. IPO & Listings

Neither the author nor the publisher assumes any responsibility or liability whatsoever on behalf of the consumer or reader of this material. Any perceived slight of any individual or organization is purely unintentional.

The resources in this book are provided for informational purposes only, and should not be used to replace the specialized training and professional judgment of investment bankers, lawyers, fund managers, or other financial and/or legal professionals. Neither the author nor the publisher can be held responsible for the use of the information provided within this book. Please always consult a trained professional before making any financial, legal, or investment decision.

For Cooperation, Consultation or Join Group, Please Contact (Tel / WhatsApp / WeChat): +1 (917) 985 7989 (U.S.); +852 5162 6310 (HK); +86 152 1081 6303 (China); Email: CEO@USFinance.Org. If You Also Wish to Publish Your Book(s) Globally, Please Contact Us or Send Us Manuscript(s). www.USFinance.Org; www.USLegal.Group

WhatsApp 　　　　WeChat 　　　　IPO DreamWorks

Capitalizing on Dreams: Guide to U.S. IPO & Listings

Introduction to the Author and the Publishers

The Author:

- **Sean Jiang**

Mr. Jiang is seasoned investment banker & fund manager (U.S., China, HK), and experienced lawyer (U.S. & China) with 20+ years' experience in U.S., HK, China, and global capital markets. He serves as the Chairman of US International Finance Foundation & China Hedge Funds Association. He is also the founder of IPO DreamWorks, the Manager Director of Xinde Financial Group, the founding partner and CEO of United Securities Legal Group, and the dean of Sunde Financial College. He has managed 1 billion+ investment funds, participated in, coordinated, and/or orchestrated many high-profile and successfully international capital market and investment deals such as: 58, Baidu, China Coal, E-Life, EDTK, China Tobacco & Alcohol, Offshore Financial Group, EDTK, EJH, MSS, Grid Dynamic, DTSS, etc. Mr. Jiang is also a successful global real estate developer.

The Publishers:

- **US International Finance Foundation ("USIFF"**, www.USFinance.Org)

Capitalizing on Dreams: Guide to U.S. IPO & Listings

USIFF is a distinguished nonprofit organization based in the U.S., committed to the advancement and promotion of the American financial industry. Established with a vision to foster innovation, excellence, and integrity within the financial sector,

USIFF plays a pivotal role in shaping the future of finance in the country and beyond. USIFF's mission at is to empower the financial community through education, research, and advocacy. USIFF strives to create an environment where financial institutions can thrive while maintaining the highest ethical standards. By setting benchmarks for financial excellence, USIFF aims to inspire a new era of responsible and sustainable growth in the industry.

Since inception, USIFF has made significant strides in promoting financial literacy, driving policy changes, and supporting the development of innovative financial solutions. USIFF's efforts have contributed to a more robust, inclusive, and dynamic financial industry that benefits all stakeholders and the world.

- **United Securities Legal Group ("US Legal Group", www.USLegal.Group)**

US Legal Group is a leading-edge law firm at the forefront of the legal industry in the U.S. With a stellar reputation for excellence, US Legal Group specializes in a diverse range of legal services that cater to the complex needs of global

Capitalizing on Dreams: Guide to U.S. IPO & Listings

clients in the dynamic world of finance, dispute resolution, IP, immigration, and beyond.

US Legal Group boasts an impressive track record of successfully handling high-profile cases and deals. Our success stories are a testament to its expertise, dedication, and the results-driven approach of legal team, which consists of seasoned attorney(s), each a leader in their respective fields, supported by a network of legal professionals who are passionate about delivering outstanding legal services.

US Legal Group invites you to join them in navigating the global legal landscapes. Whether you're seeking legal counsel for a single issue or require ongoing legal support, US Legal Group is ready to serve you with the highest standard of professionalism and expertise.

The Sponsors:

"*IPO DreamWorks Series*" books are honored to be sponsored by the following entities:

- **China Listed Companies Association**
- **Manhattan Securities Group**
- **China International Finance Foundation**
- **InterContinental Financial Group**

Capitalizing on Dreams: Guide to U.S. IPO & Listings

- Xinde Asset Management Group

- Guo Huan Law Firm (China Renowned Law Firm)

- China Tobacco and Alcohol Group

- Offshore Financial Group

The Contributors:

The author and the publishers would like to express their sincere appreciation to Joyce Guo, Jenny Zhang, Fidy Hong, Simon Cao, etc., who have provided invaluable expert advices and technical supports that greatly enhanced the accuracy and depth of this book in the writing process of the *IPO DreamWorks Series*.

WhatsApp   **WeChat**   **IPO DreamWorks**

Capitalizing on Dreams: Guide to U.S. IPO & Listings

Table of Contents

1. Embarking on the IPO Adventure: A Journey into the Public Realm 17
2. A Glimpse into the IPO World 19
    2.1   Unlocking the Treasure Trove: The Allure of Going Public 19
    2.2   The Flip Side of the Coin: Delving into the Disadvantages of Going Public 21
    2.3   The Cast of Characters in the Great IPO Spectacle 26
    2.4   The Prelude to the IPO: Timing Your Underwriter Courtship 29
    2.5   Selecting the Maestro for Your IPO Symphony: What to Look for in a Managing Underwriter 32
    2.6   Setting the Stage for Your IPO: The First Steps After Choosing a Managing Underwriter 35
    2.7   The Art of Underwriting: Exploring the Different Approaches to Taking Your Company Public 37
    2.8   The Art of Pricing: Unlocking the Value of Your Company's Shares 39
    2.9   The IPO Shares Dilemma: How Many to Offer? 41
    2.10   Crafting the Canvas: A Guide to Preparing a Registration Statement 44
    2.11   The Great Unveiling: A Playful Probe into Due Diligence 46
    2.12   The SEC's Role in the IPO Drama: A Play by Play   50

2.13 A Garden of Opportunities: The "Emerging Growth Company" and the JOBS Act..............52
2.14 Stealth Mode: Filing with the SEC Under the Radar 54
2.15 The Roadshow: A Theatrical Tour of Your Company's Story..............57
2.16 The FINRA Finale: Ensuring Compliance for a Curtain Call..............59
2.17 The Big Stage: How Your Stock Takes Center Stage on a National Stock Exchange..............61
2.18 The Pledge of Commitment: Signing the Underwriting Agreement..............63
2.19 The Underwriters' Reward: A Play on Profit....64
2.20 Unlocking the Payday: When the Shares and Money Change Hands..............65
2.21 The Consequences of Missteps: Material Misstatements and Omissions in the Registration Statement..............67

3. CORPORATE HOUSEKEEPING..............71
3.1 The Art of Recapitalization: Setting the Stage for an IPO 71
3.2 The Grand Conversion: Preferred Securities Before the IPO Curtain Rises..............73
3.3 Readying the Stage: Is Your Company's Structure Suited for Public Eyes?..............74
3.4 Charter Tweaks: Polishing the Corporate Blueprint for the IPO Spotlight..............75
3.5 Bylaws Buff Up: Getting House Rules IPO-Ready 77
3.6 Leading the IPO Parade: Management's Key

Duties in the Planning and Prep Phases..................79
3.7 Polishing the Corporate Crown: Governance Touch-Ups Before the IPO Curtain 81
3.8 Setting the Stage for Independence: The Role of Independent Directors 83
3.9 The Essential Cast of Committees: Crafting the Board's Supporting Roles..................84
3.10 Embracing the Script of Ethics: Crafting a Code for Company Leaders 86
3.11 Safeguarding the Guardians: Shielding Directors and Officers from Liability 89
3.12 Navigating the Numbers: Preparing for Accounting Challenges in an IPO..................91
3.13 Choosing the Right Auditor for Your IPO Journey 93
3.14 Auditor Eligibility Under Sarbanes-Oxley: A Checklist for Compliance..................95
3.15 Spotlight on IPO Accounting: Navigating Key Concerns 96
3.16 Fortifying the Bulwarks: Preparing for Takeover Defenses in an IPO..................99
3.17 Aligning Employment Agreements with Public Standards: A Pre-IPO Checklist 103
3.18 Refining the Employee Benefit Plan for an IPO: A Strategic Overview..................105
3.19 Equipping for Success: Crafting New Equity Compensation Plans Pre-IPO 107
3.20 Shareholder Nods for Equity Plans..................110
4. The Art of Public Communication During the IPO Registration Process..................111

Capitalizing on Dreams: Guide to U.S. IPO & Listings

4.1 Navigating the Quiet Seas: Understanding Gun-Jumping 111
4.2 The Silent Prelude: Unveiling the "Quiet Period" in Finance 113
4.3 Whispers in the Wind: Navigating the Communication Boundaries of the Quiet Period 114
4.4 Leaping Too Soon: The Consequences of SEC's Gun-Jumping 116
4.5 Navigating the Quiet Waters: Safe Harbors for Communications in the Pre-Filing Period 117
4.6 The Quiet Before the Storm: The Waiting Period Explained 120
4.7 The Art of Marketing Under Wraps: Restrictions on Written Materials During the Waiting Period 120
4.8 The Fine Art of Verbal Pitching: Navigating Oral Marketing Restrictions During the Waiting Period 122
4.9 Steering Clear of Spotlights: General Publicity During the Waiting Period 123
4.10 Crafting the Cryptic Call: Designing a "Tombstone Ad" Amidst the Waiting Period 124
4.11 The Digital Stage: Unveiling the Internet Roadshow 126
4.12 Engaging Digitally: Handling Bulletin Boards and Chat Rooms During the Waiting Period 127
4.13 Safeguarding Against Violations: Precautions During the Registration Period 127
5. On Going Disclosure Obligations and Requirements 131
5.1 Essential Filings: A Concise Guide to SEC Documents 131
5.2 Fiduciary Duties of Officers in Periodic

Reporting: An In-Depth Look 136
5.3   Consequences of Non-Compliance: A Look at the Penalties for Violating SEC Certification Requirements 139
5.4   Unstructured Disclosure Obligations: The Dynamics of Material Events and Communication 141
5.5   Regulation FD and Analyst Communications: Ensuring Fair Disclosure 144
5.6   Dancing with Regulation FD: A Playful Guide to Compliance 146
5.7   The High Stakes of Skipping the Regulation FD Waltz: A Look at the Consequences 149
5.8   Guarding the Garden: Preventive Measures Against Insider Trading 151
5.9   The Heavy Hand of Justice: Penalties for Securities Fraud Unveiled 154
5.10   The Playbook of Integrity: Navigating the Foreign Corrupt Practices Act 156
5.11   Tiptoeing Through the Tulips: A Whimsical Look at Insider Trading Regulations 158
5.12   The Symphony of Section 16: A Playful Guide to SEC Filings 160
5.13   The Whirlwind of Section 16(b): A Lighthearted Look at Short-Swing Profits 162
5.14   Tiptoeing Through the Tulips: Insider Trading and Short Sales 165
5.15   The Grand Reveal: Unveiling Significant Shareholders' Reporting Chore 166
5.16   Unlocking the Vault: Insider Share Sales Post-IPO   168

5.17 Unlocking the Insider's Share Sale Safari: A Rule 144 Expedition 171
5.18 Can Employees Cash in on Pre-IPO Shares? A Quick Jaunt Through Rule 701 and Rule 144 174
5.19 SOX Safari: Crafting a Public Company's Document Trail 176
5.20 The Grand Adventure of Document Retention 177
5.21 Preserve and Protect: The Document Duty Dance 178
5.22 The High Stakes Game of Document Destruction: A Cautionary Tale 179
5.23 Crafting a Risk-Ready Business 181
5.24 SOX in a Nutshell: The Sarbanes-Oxley Act Explained 183
5.25 The Sarbanes-Oxley Act and Loans to Company Stewards 184
5.26 SOX's Audit Committee Standards: A Concise Guide 186
5.27 The Audit Committee: Guardians of Auditor Independence 188
5.28 SOX Whistleblower Provisions: Shielding the Corporate Watchdogs 190
5.29 Empowerment of the Audit Committee: Hiring Outside Advisors 191
5.30 SOX Requirements for Disclosure Controls and Financial Reporting 192
5.31 SOX and Non-GAAP Measures: The New Disclosure Paradigm 195
5.32 Presenting Non-GAAP Financial Information: A Guide to Compliance 197

5.33 Oral Non-GAAP Disclosures: Navigating Regulation G Compliance 200
5.34 Regulation G and Earnings Releases: A Compliance Overview 202
5.35 Off-Balance Sheet Financing Disclosure: Unveiling the Invisible 204
5.36 Audit Influence and Liability: The SEC's Stance 207
5.37 Clawback Provisions of SOX: A Safety Net for Financial Integrity 209
5.38 SOX's Broad Reach: Implications for Directors and Officers 210
5.39 Dodd-Frank Act: A Sea Change in Financial Regulation 212
Appendix A: Sample Timetable for an IPO and Listing of Common Stocks on NASDAQ or NYSE 215

For Cooperation, Consultation or Join Group, Please Contact (Tel / WhatsApp / WeChat): +1 (917) 985 7989 (U.S.); +852 5162 6310 (HK); +86 152 1081 6303 (China); Email: CEO@USFinance.Org. If You Also Wish to Publish Your Book(s) Globally, Please Contact Us or Send Us Manuscript(s).
www.USFinance.Org; www.USLegal.Group

Capitalizing on Dreams: Guide to U.S. IPO & Listings

For Cooperation, Consultation or Join Group, Please Contact (Tel / WhatsApp / WeChat): +1 (917) 985 7989 (U.S.); +852 5162 6310 (HK); +86 152 1081 6303 (China); Email: CEO@USFinance.Org. If You Also Wish to Publish Your Book(s) Globally, Please Contact Us or Send Us Manuscript(s).

WhatsApp   WeChat   IPO DreamWorks

Capitalizing on Dreams: Guide to U.S. IPO & Listings

Capitalizing on Dreams: Guide to U.S. IPO & Listings

CHAPTER ONE

1. Embarking on the IPO Adventure: A Journey into the Public Realm

Imagine a moment of transformation, where a company steps out from the shadows of private ownership into the bright lights of the public stage. That's right, we're talking about an Initial Public Offering ("**IPO**") – a dazzling debut where a company's shares make their first appearance to the world at large. It's like a grand entrance at a high-profile gala, where the company is the belle of the ball, and the public is the eager audience.

Why would a company want to go public? Well, it's all about growth, my friend. Raising capital is like planting seeds for future expansion. It's also a way to pay off debts, which is like tidying up the attic before hosting a party. And let's not forget liquidity for shareholders – it's like giving them a ticket to the financial amusement park.

Going public is a rite of passage, especially in the era of corporate reform under the Sarbanes-Oxley Act ("**SOX**"). It's a bit like graduating from a school of corporate excellence.

But hold on to your hats, because an IPO is a thrilling rollercoaster ride that can be quite the workout for a company's management team. It's like training for a marathon – you've got to be prepared for the long haul and the

Capitalizing on Dreams: Guide to U.S. IPO & Listings

regulatory hurdles that come with it. The Securities and Exchange Commission ("**SEC**") is like the referee of this race, ensuring everyone plays by the rules.

Now, every company's journey is unique, like snowflakes or your favorite pair of jeans, but the basic steps to going public are like a well-rehearsed dance.

US International Finance Foundation & United Securities Legal Group are here to be your guide on this exhilarating expedition. We're like the sherpas in the Himalayas, ready to help you navigate the peaks and valleys of the IPO process. We aim to demystify the going-public experience and prepare you for the new horizons that await once your company's securities are out there for all to see.

While we can't predict every twist and turn your company will face during its IPO, we can certainly map out the key players, their roles, and the general path you'll be taking. Think of this as your treasure map, but instead of X marking the spot, it's the SEC's stamp of approval.

WhatsApp   **WeChat**   **IPO DreamWorks**

Capitalizing on Dreams: Guide to U.S. IPO & Listings

CHAPTER TWO

2. A Glimpse into the IPO World

This primer is your ticket to understanding the cast of characters in the going-public play, their roles, and the grand performance itself. For a step-by-step backstage pass, flip to Appendix A, where we've laid out a detailed timeline of the IPO – it's like a script for the big show, complete with cues and stage directions.

So, are you ready to take the curtain call? Let's make your company's IPO a performance to remember!

2.1 Unlocking the Treasure Trove: The Allure of Going Public

Ahoy, shareholders! Ready to set sail for the open seas of public trading? Going public is like discovering a hidden cove of financial opportunities, brimming with advantages that can transform your company's landscape.

(a) Navigating the Liquidity Lagoon

First up, the waters of liquidity. By casting your net into the public market, you're not only catching fish, but you're catching the ability to sell your shares with ease. Before, your investment was like a sunken treasure chest, hard to reach and harder to sell. Now, with a public listing, you can trade your shares in a bustling marketplace, albeit with some rules of the game to keep in mind, like the SEC's Rule 144.

(b) Diving into the Deep Pockets of Immediate Funds

Next, let's talk about the treasure chest of funds you can immediately unlock. The average haul from public offerings since 2001 has been a cool $110 million, with some lucky finds exceeding the billion mark. This cash is like a genie's lamp, ready to grant your company's wishes, be it for working capital, debt repayment, or even a daring acquisition.

(c) Sailing the Seas of Capital Access

Ah, the winds of finance! Public companies find themselves with a favorable breeze, as they can tap into a broader ocean of financing options. If your stock makes a splash in the market, you might find yourself raising additional funds on favorable terms, expanding your financial horizons.

(d) Charting the Course for Talent

Now, let's hoist the sails for your crew. Publicly traded stock can be the golden lure in your talent acquisition net. Stock options can be a siren's song to management and employees, enhancing your company's allure and helping you hold onto your star performers.

(e) Conquering New Territories with Acquisitions

Ah, the conquests! With the spoils from an IPO, you can not only buy out other companies with cash but also offer your now-coveted stock as currency. This way, you can expand your empire without emptying your coffers.

(f) Basking in the Prestige of Public Ownership

The glow of prestige awaits you on the public stage. Being a publicly traded company can elevate your company's status, making it a beacon in the business world. Your customers and suppliers might even become shareholders, rooting for your success with every purchase.

(g) Wealth for the Wise Investors

Lastly, the wealth of the wise. A public offering can be a boon for the net worth of those who own closely-held companies. Even if immediate profits aren't on the horizon, the ability to use publicly traded stock as collateral opens doors to new ventures and opportunities.

So, are you ready to raise the anchor and set sail towards the public markets? The winds are favorable, and the seas are full of promise!

2.2 The Flip Side of the Coin: Delving into the Disadvantages

Capitalizing on Dreams: Guide to U.S. IPO & Listings of Going Public

Ah, the allure of the public markets—like a siren's song, they call with promises of wealth and fame. But beware, dear captain of industry, for there be dragons in these waters. Let's hoist the Jolly Roger and explore the hidden reefs and treacherous currents that could dash your company's dreams on the rocky shores of reality.

(a) The High Seas of Expenditure

Prepare to loosen the purse strings, for the journey to the public markets is not for the faint of heart—or wallet. The initial foray into an IPO can set you back a hefty sum, with underwriter commissions typically ranging from 4% to 7%. And that's just the tip of the iceberg; the iceberg being the average expenses of over $ 1.5 - 2 million, which include a veritable pirate's treasure trove of fees: legal, accounting, printing, transfer agent, SEC registration, and stock exchange listing.

Once you've weathered that storm, the ongoing tempest of federal regulatory reporting will demand a hefty annual tribute in administrative, legal, and accounting costs. The Sarbanes-Oxley winds blow strongest here, with smaller companies (meaning companies with under $700 million of annual revenue) bracing for an 0.8 million annual compliance costs, while larger companies average compliance costs of over 5 million per year.

Capitalizing on Dreams: Guide to U.S. IPO & Listings

(a) The Time-Sucking Maelstrom of Management

As the captain of your company, you'll find yourself at the helm of a ship that demands constant navigation through the treacherous straits of the IPO process, a journey that can last up to six months. And once you've reached the shores of public ownership, the seas of shareholder relations and public disclosure require a constant vigil.

(b) The Burdensome Ballast of Compliance

Once you've hoisted the Jolly Roger of public trading, the federal securities laws will weigh you down with the requirement to disclose a vast array of information. This treasure map of data must be updated annually and quarterly, with certain X-marked spots needing to be revealed the moment they're discovered.

The ship must be tightly rigged with controls and procedures to ensure the timely release of information, and the captain (management) must personally vouch for the accuracy of the charts (periodic reports). The Sarbanes-Oxley Act demands a personal log entry (internal control report) and an audit by an independent quartermaster (auditor), which can be both costly and disruptive to the ship's daily voyage.

(c) The Exposed Decks of Public Scrutiny

The initial prospectus and subsequent filings with the SEC will strip your company bare, revealing intimate details that were once cloaked in secrecy. This exposure can arm competitors with knowledge they would not otherwise possess, potentially giving them the upper hand in the cutthroat waters of commerce.

(d) The Shark-Infested Waters of Liability

Going public casts a wide net that can snare officers and directors in the jaws of liability. The requirement to broadcast material information opens the door to second-guessing from analysts, the press, and shareholders. And with the rise of law firms specializing in securities class actions, officers and directors may find themselves in the crosshairs of litigation if the company's stock takes a nosedive.

(e) The Chains of Insider Restrictions

Federal securities laws shackle the ability of "insiders" to freely trade their shares, with a strict code (Rule 144) dictating when and how they can sell. Insiders must also navigate the treacherous waters of Section 16(b) and Rule 10b-5, which impose penalties for trading on the basis of nonpublic information.

(f) The Diminishing Incentive of Stock Options

While stock options can be a powerful lure for

performance and retention when private, once the profits are realized, they may lose their potency. Proxy advisory firms like ISS are on the prowl for compensation they deem excessive, and accounting standards have changed, requiring public companies to expense stock options and equity awards.

(g) The Anchor of Management Flexibility

The anchor of public ownership can drag down the agility of management decisions. There are practical constraints on salaries, benefits, and other operating procedures, and the composition and responsibilities of the board of directors are subject to stringent requirements.

(h) The Siren Song of Stock Price Concerns

The melody of the stock price can become a siren song, leading management to chase short-term profits at the expense of long-term strategy, a dangerous dance that can lead to unsound business decisions.

(i) The Perilous Waters of Control

Existing shareholders face the immediate dilution of their ownership, and in the long run, the risk of losing control or facing an unfriendly takeover. While defensive measures can be taken, they may not find favor with underwriters or potential shareholders.

(j) The Constant Storm of Growth and Profit Pressure

Finally, the relentless pressure to maintain growth and profit levels can turn the voyage into a frantic race against time. The quarterly reporting of operating results can intensify this pressure, narrowing the management's planning and operating horizons and potentially leading to short-term decisions with long-term consequences.

So, dear captain, as you chart your course towards the public markets, be wary of the hidden shoals and treacherous currents that lie beneath the glittering surface. With caution and wisdom, you may yet navigate these waters to find the treasure you seek.

2.3 The Cast of Characters in the Great IPO Spectacle

In the grand theater of an Initial Public Offering (IPO), a colorful cast of characters plays pivotal roles in orchestrating this financial blockbuster. Let's peer behind the curtain and meet the ensemble that brings the show to life.

(a) The Star of the Show: The Company

The protagonist, known by many monikers such as 'issuer,' 'registrant,' or simply 'the company,' is the one stepping into the limelight. This is the entity whose shares are about to take center stage in the public market.

(b) Supporting Actors: Selling Shareholders

These are the shareholders who, with the blessing of the underwriters, are ready to part with their shares in this grand event. They are eager to cash in their tickets to financial freedom.

(c) The Director's Chair: Management

Deep in the heart of the action, the management team dons multiple hats. They are the scriptwriters of the 'due diligence' information, the leads in Q&A sessions, and the dramatists in drafting the registration statement. Their ability to pitch the IPO is the secret sauce to the show's success.

(d) The Board of Directors

These are the seasoned advisors, required to unveil their own stories, their business sagas, and their ties to the company. They put their John Hancock on the registration statement, lending their gravitas to the proceedings.

(e) The Master of Ceremonies: Underwriters

The managing underwriter(s) take center stage, orchestrating the IPO's symphony. They craft the corporate financing structure, pen the prospectus, and set the tempo for the offering and share price. They are the ringmasters of the roadshow, the architects of the syndicate, and the mentors for post-show support.

(f) The Scriptwriters: Issuer's Counsel

The issuer's counsel is the wordsmith, crafting the registration statement alongside the management and underwriters. They navigate the SEC's review process and help the company prepare for its new role as a public entity, ensuring all legal i's are dotted and t's crossed.

(g) The Legal Mavericks: Underwriters' Counsel

These legal tacticians conduct their own due diligence, draft and negotiate the underwriting agreement, and ensure all is in order for the curtain call. They coordinate filings and make sure the show doesn't break any securities laws.

(h) The Specialized Consultants: Patent/Regulatory Counsel

In industries where expertise is key, these consultants provide insights and draft sections of the registration statement. They may even offer their expert opinions to the underwriters on certain matters, adding a layer of credibility to the show.

(i) The Financial Accountants: Auditors

These number-crunchers audit the financial statements and the effectiveness of the company's internal controls.

They assist in penning the 'MD&A' section and address any accounting queries from the SEC, culminating in the delivery of the 'comfort letter,' a critical part of the underwriters' due diligence.

(j) **The Printers of Prosperity: Financial Printer**

As the registration statement nears its final draft, the financial printer takes over, mass-producing the preliminary and final prospectus for the audience of investors. They also prepare the electronic version for submission via the SEC's EDGAR system.

(k) **The Ensemble of Experts**

Depending on the company's needs, a variety of other experts may join the troupe. From designers of stock certificates to insurance agents and transfer agents, each plays a part in ensuring the IPO's smooth performance. And let's not forget the public relations consultants, who help shape the company's narrative for the public eye.

In this financial extravaganza, each player, from the star to the supporting cast, contributes to the spectacle that is an IPO. With careful choreography and teamwork, they aim to make this show a hit on the public stage.

2.4 The Prelude to the IPO: Timing Your Underwriter Courtship

Capitalizing on Dreams: Guide to U.S. IPO & Listings

Picture this: your company is the star of an upcoming show, and the underwriters are the seasoned producers who can turn your performance into a box office hit. But when should the curtain rise on this critical courtship?

The answer is a resounding "the sooner, the better." The selection of an underwriter is akin to choosing a dance partner for a performance that could make or break your company's debut on the public stage. It's a process that should commence at least six months, and possibly a year, before the offering is set to dazzle the audience.

(a) The Art of Courtship

Think of this period as a grand courtship. You'll want to take your time, meeting and interviewing several firms, each vying to be your company's leading man or woman. As you size them up, they'll be doing the same, assessing your company's star quality and its potential to shine as a public entity.

This extended period of wooing allows both parties to develop a rapport, to understand each other's steps and strategies. It's about building trust in the underwriters' judgment, competence, commitment, and integrity—qualities as essential as a sturdy stage in a theater.

(b) Selling Your Story

By initiating early discussions, you give yourself the

chance to tell your company's story, chapter by chapter, over time. You can showcase your growth, your upward-trending budgets, your innovative product developments, and your shining results, all of which help to build your credibility with the underwriters.

(c) Choosing the Leading Underwriter

In the end, you'll be seeking out the managing underwriters for your offering. The lead underwriter, whose name takes the spotlight on the bottom left of the prospectus cover, will typically take the helm of the operation. They'll assemble a syndicate, a troupe of other investment banking firms, to assist in selling the securities.

As you near the final act of choosing your underwriters, ensure you meet the key players in the organization—the maestro of the syndicate department, the virtuoso of institutional sales, the conductor of your company's stock trading, the impresario of the office, and the corporate finance team who will be your co-stars in this offering.

(d) Finding the Right Fit

Get a sense of their philosophy, their approach to the business, and ensure there's a philosophical alignment, as well as a business synergy. After all, you want to ensure that when the curtains rise, you're not just ready to perform, but you're performing with partners who share your vision and passion for success.

In essence, the earlier you start the discussions with underwriters, the better prepared you'll be to step into the limelight with confidence and a strong supporting cast.

2.5 Selecting the Maestro for Your IPO Symphony: What to Look for in a Managing Underwriter

Embarking on the journey to go public is like composing a grand symphony. The managing underwriter is the maestro who waves the baton, guiding the orchestra through the intricate movements of your Initial Public Offering (IPO). But what qualities should you seek in this conductor of capital?

(a) The Maestro's Experience

First and foremost, does this maestro have a proven track record in your industry's melodies and the specific instruments of securities you wish to play? Examine their past performances—how many were priced on pitch within the original range, and what was the completion rate of their shows? How have their past productions fared in the aftermarket? Request a program of their last 10 offerings and delve into the stories behind any that were cancelled. Reach out to the performers from those shows for candid feedback on the maestro's leadership, support, and the harmony they provided before, during, and after the performance.

(b) Reputation Resonates

Consider the underwriter's reputation, both as a general impresario and within the niche of your industry. Your company will be linked to their brand, so choose a maestro with a strong reputation among institutional and retail investors. They should be respected by their peers, capable of assembling a robust ensemble to sell and distribute the stock.

(c) Distribution Dynamo

The maestro's ability to control and influence the distribution channels is crucial. They must generate sufficient market interest to sell out your offering. In a bustling 'boom' market, this may seem easy, but in quieter times, a strong underwriter can make the difference between a standing ovation and an empty hall.

(d) After-Performance Support

Remember, the curtain doesn't close when the offering is complete. The underwriter continues to support the performance as a market-maker, purchaser, analyst, and facilitator, ensuring your stock's success **post**-show. The company needs a deep, liquid, and orderly market, which requires well-capitalized market makers, especially the managing underwriter and their assembled syndicate.

(e) Analyst Applause

The underwriter's analysts should be well-versed in your industry and respected in the investment community. A strong research department can help position your company effectively and provide insightful **early** reports. Investigate the analysts' reputations and their relationships with your competitors.

(f) Capital for Growth

As your company matures, it may need to raise additional capital. Choose an underwriter with the capacity to grow with you and a history of successful offerings to bolster your company's future fundraising **efforts**.

(g) Ongoing Oracle

Your company may require ongoing advice on a wide array of financial matters. An investment banker with whom you've built a relationship can be a valuable source of guidance, with some underwriters offering a broader range of **services** than others.

(h) Terms and Conditions

Finally, consider the contractual fine print. How flexible are they with the number of shares current owners can sell? What are the lock-up requirements? How are expenses allocated in success or failure? Do they share your company's valuation assessment?

In selecting your managing underwriter, you're not just choosing a partner for one performance but potentially for many future encores. Ensure they not only have the expertise and reputation but also the philosophy and commitment to help your company's story resonate with the audience of investors.

2.6 Setting the Stage for Your IPO: The First Steps After Choosing a Managing Underwriter

With the managing underwriter by your side, it's time to step into the wings and prepare for the IPO performance. The curtain rises on the first act with an organizational meeting, a crucial gathering that sets the stage for all that follows.

(a) The Grand Meeting: Organizing the Troops

Once the decision to go public is made, the managing underwriter usually orchestrates an organizational meeting. This meeting serves as a grand introduction, aligning the key players and mapping out the strategic timetable for the IPO. It's designed to be a well-timed schedule that accommodates due diligence, registration statement preparation, SEC review, and commentary, culminating in a "roadshow" that avoids the off-peak marketing seasons.

(b) The Three Acts of the Meeting

The organizational meeting typically unfolds in three acts:

- **The Overview**: A discussion of the offering's size, timeline, and mechanics, where responsibilities are allocated like roles in a play.

- **The Company's Narrative**: A concise overview by the company of its business and affairs, setting the scene for the IPO story.

- **The Discussion**: An open dialogue among parties to address any significant issues that have been identified, a collaborative brainstorming session.

(c) Telling Your Company's Story

For the company, this meeting is the first of many storytelling sessions. The narrative presented is brief but sets the tone for the IPO team. It lays down the broad themes that will be the script for the business description in the prospectus and the oral presentations during the roadshow. This story will be the foundation for all future communications post-IPO, including analysts' meetings, press releases, and periodic reports.

(d) Due Diligence and Issue Identification

The organizational meeting is also an ideal time for the company to bring forth any issues that could influence the offering process. It's wise for the company to have several pre-meeting sessions with counsel and accountants to anticipate potential challenges. Underwriters value transparency, as it allows them time to navigate these issues and builds trust with the management team.

(e) Preparation and Proactivity

When significant issues surface later in the due diligence process, it can cause delays or even halt the IPO. Therefore, it's expected that underwriters and their counsel come prepared to the organizational meeting, having researched the company, its industry, regulatory landscape, and market potential.

In essence, the first step after selecting a managing underwriter is to embark on a collaborative journey that begins with a well-organized meeting. This sets the pace for a successful IPO, ensuring that everyone is on the same page, working towards a harmonious and well-executed public offering.

2.7 The Art of Underwriting: Exploring the Different Approaches to Taking Your Company Public

When it comes to the grand performance of an Initial Public Offering (IPO), the managing underwriter can propose one of two main types of underwriting arrangements, each with its own script and set of stage directions.

(a) Firm Commitment Underwriting: The Star Role

In this type of underwriting, the underwriter steps into the spotlight, agreeing to purchase the entire issue of securities. This means they take on the starring role and the risk for any unsold shares. From the company's perspective, this is the preferred option and the most commonly used method in the world of IPOs.

The underwriter's commitment is sealed at the moment the offering price is determined, which happens just before the curtain rises on the effective time of the prospectus. This timing allows the issue to be priced according to the current mood of the market, ensuring that the offering resonates with investors.

(b) Best Efforts Underwriting: The Supporting Act

In contrast, best efforts underwriting is like a supporting role on stage. Here, the underwriting firm pledges to use their best efforts to sell the issue, but they are not obligated to buy any unsold securities. It's a promise to give it their all, but without the full commitment of taking on the entire production.

The Choice of Underwriting: A Strategic Decision The choice between firm commitment and best efforts underwriting is a strategic decision that depends on the company's confidence in the market's reception and the underwriter's assessment of the potential for success.

Firm Commitment: The Preferred Path For most companies embarking on the IPO journey, the firm commitment underwriting is the preferred path. It offers a sense of security, knowing that the underwriter is fully invested in the success of the offering, working hand in hand with the company to ensure that the performance is a hit with the audience of investors.

In summary, while the firm commitment underwriting is the star of the show in the IPO world, understanding the different types of underwriting is crucial for companies to make an informed decision that aligns with their goals and risk tolerance. Whether it's the full commitment of a firm underwriting or the dedicated effort of a best efforts arrangement, the right choice can help set the stage for a successful public debut.

2.8 The Art of Pricing: Unlocking the Value of Your Company's Shares

Pricing the stock for an Initial Public Offering (IPO) is a delicate dance, a balance between the company's aspirations and the market's appetite. Here's how the stage is set for determining the price range of your company's soon-to-be-public shares.

(a) Setting the Preliminary Range

At the beginning of the act, the underwriters and the

company agree on a tentative range of prices. This range is a starting point, a melody that will be refined as the process unfolds, with the precise note of the share price being struck just before the offering begins. This timing allows the price to resonate with the current market tune and the feedback from potential investors.

(b) The Role of Market Dynamics

Remember, the market is the ultimate conductor, setting the final price for the issue. While underwriters may provide early indications or promises, these are not set in stone. Once the upfront costs are incurred, the company often has to align with the market's valuation, even if it differs from earlier suggestions.

(c) Striking the Right Note

The highest price may seem like the ultimate goal, but it's not always the most harmonious choice. Satisfying future investors is key; an overpriced offering could lead to immediate discontent if the price falls post-IPO. Savvy underwriters often price an issue just below the peak to allow for a modest increase post-offering, creating goodwill and a buffer against short-term market fluctuations.

(d) Balancing Dual Loyalties

It's important to remember that underwriters serve two

clients: the company and their investors. They must balance the interests of both, aiming for a price that satisfies the company's valuation while also appealing to the investor's sense of value.

(e) The Moment Before the Curtain Rises

Once the registration statement takes effect and the deal is priced—signing the underwriting agreement as the final note—the stock trading is set to commence the next morning.

(f) The Syndicate's Pre-Opening Prelude

Before the market opens, the syndicate sales force may reach out to customers to confirm sales, ensuring that the stage is set for a smooth opening day of trading.

In essence, determining the price range for your IPO is about finding the sweet spot where the company's value meets the market's demand. It's a collaborative effort with the underwriters, requiring a deep understanding of the market, the company's story, and the investors' expectations. By getting this right, you set the tone for a successful public listing and lay the foundation for a positive relationship with your new shareholders.

2.9 The IPO Shares Dilemma: How Many to Offer?

Deciding how many shares to sell in an IPO is a bit like

planning a feast—you want to serve enough to satisfy your guests but not so much that there's a surplus that goes to waste. Here's how to get the portions right.

(a) Pre-Organizational Meeting Planning

Before the organizational meeting, engage in a dialogue with your managing underwriters to determine the capital your company aims to raise and how many new shares this will entail. Remember, the menu of intended fund uses must be disclosed in the prospectus.

(b) Valuation and Share Calculation

The underwriter's valuation and the number of existing shares, post any pre-IPO recapitalizations, will help calculate the approximate number of new shares, known as "primary shares," needed to meet your fundraising goals.

(c) Secondary Shares Consideration

Also, consider whether current shareholders will sell part of their stake, known as "secondary shares." The total offering size is the sum of primary and secondary shares. The underwriter may recommend recapitalization to position the share price in a marketable range.

(d) Historical Share Allocation

Historically, the number of primary shares in an IPO has averaged between 15% and 25% of a company's total shares on a fully diluted basis. Including secondary shares is subject to marketing constraints, and underwriters often advise against it to avoid negative perceptions from potential investors.

(e) Float Factor

Consider the "float"—the number of shares available for public trading post-IPO. A larger float typically means greater liquidity, while a smaller float can mean higher volatility. Institutional investors often have minimum float requirements for the securities they purchase.

(f) Marketability and Float Guidance

The managing underwriter will guide you on the desirable float size to market the securities effectively. They usually aim for an IPO that creates a float valued at 40–50 million to ensure a liquid market post-IPO.

(g) Other Determining Factors

Other factors include the capital's intended use, the dilution effect on existing shareholders, and the potential impact on earnings per share (EPS).

(h) The Over-Allotment Option

Much like an emergency plan or "plan B", most firm commitment underwritings include an over-allotment option, colloquially known as the "green shoe" option. This allows the underwriters a 30-day option to purchase additional shares, typically 15% of the offering size, to meet excess demand, thereby supporting the IPO's success.

In essence, deciding how many shares to sell in an IPO is about striking a balance between meeting your capital needs and creating a marketable, liquid offering that appeals to investors and supports your company's long-term growth. With careful planning and guidance from your underwriters, you can size your offering to make the most of your public debut.

2.10 Crafting the Canvas: A Guide to Preparing a Registration Statement

The registration statement is the artist's palette for an IPO—it's where the vision of your company comes to life for potential investors. Let's break down the process of preparing this critical document.

(a) The Two-Act Play: Parts I and II

The registration statement is composed of two acts. Act I, or Part I, is the prospectus—the main event that gets distributed to the public. It's the narrative that tells your company's story, including its business, risks, and plans for the IPO proceeds. Act II, or Part II, offers behind-the-scenes insights available for public inspection, including material contracts and more.

(b) The Scriptwriting Process

Typically, the company and its legal counsel draft the initial script of the registration statement. The document follows a customary sequence, starting with an overview of the business, followed by the underwriting plan, capitalization details, and more.

(c) The Star Characters: MD&A and CD&A

Two key characters in this play are the Management's Discussion and Analysis (MD&A) and the Compensation Discussion and Analysis (CD&A). The MD&A offers investors a backstage pass to the company's financial thought process, while the CD&A sheds light on the compensation landscape for executives.

(d) The Common Form: Form S-1

Most companies use Form S-1 as their script template, which weaves together the registration requirements with references to Regulations S-K and S-X, which dictate the disclosure of non-financial and financial information, respectively.

(e) Balancing Act: Selling vs. Disclosing

The registration statement serves a dual purpose. It's both a sales pitch to charm investors and a disclosure document to protect the company from liability. Striking a balance can be tricky. It's common to lean towards a conservative portrayal, avoiding overly positive language and predictions that might not age well.

(f) Rehearsals and Revisions

After the first draft is circulated, the working group will meet for several read-throughs and revisions. The goal is to create a prospectus that paints an accurate and thorough picture of the company, with the underwriters' guidance to ensure the company is well-positioned in the market.

(g) Plain English, Please

Remember the SEC's "plain English" rule throughout the drafting process. This rule is like a director's guidance to actors—keep it simple, clear, and understandable. Use short sentences, active voice, and visual aids like tables and bullet points. Avoid industry jargon and convoluted phrasing.

In essence, preparing a registration statement is about transparently showcasing your company's story while also being mindful of the regulatory requirements and the need to appeal to investors. With careful drafting and revisions, you can ensure that your registration statement is both a compelling narrative and a compliant document.

2.11 The Great Unveiling: A Playful Probe into Due Diligence

Picture due diligence as a grand treasure hunt, where the treasure is truth and the chest is the company's inner workings. It's a spirited investigation that sweeps through the corridors of corporate knowledge to gather gems of information for the registration statement. This quest ensures that the prospectus glistens with accuracy and that there's not a single misrepresentation or omission hiding in the shadows. And for this adventure, the management must be as candid as can be, for the success of the mission hinges on their full disclosure.

The journey of due diligence is a sprinter's race, typically completed within the first 60 days. It's a test of time, patience, and a team spirit that gets everyone working together. By the end, the underwriters will have a treasure map that helps them guide investors through the company's riches, avoiding the booby traps of misrepresentations and omissions.

(a) The Inquisitive Start

The quest begins with a barrage of interviews, where the management is quizzed on the company's business, products, finances, and risks—think of it as a masterclass in company insights. The underwriters and their legal team are the eager students, asking questions that help them see the company in full color.

(b) The Document Expedition

Along with the interviews, the underwriters' counsel will send out a scavenger list for corporate documents, from the articles of incorporation to the minutes of board meetings, and a detailed ledger of the company's history, shareholder registry, and more. It's like gathering the pieces of a puzzle that, when put together, reveal the full picture.

(c) The Online Repository

All the gathered wisdom is then safely stored in an online data room, a digital fortress where only the chosen few can access the trove of due diligence materials, ensuring speed and efficiency in the process.

(d) The Deep Dive

The underwriters' counsel will then don their detective hats and scrutinize the company's intellectual property and assets, financials, insurance, legal battles, and tax reports. They'll also check if the company is ready to comply with the Sarbanes-Oxley Act once it takes the public stage.

(e) The Employment Audit

They'll review the company's employment status, from

the employee roster to the organizational chart, benefit plans, and union activities. This part of the investigation may even include meetings with auditors, lawyers, and sometimes even customers, turning over every stone to find the truth.

(f) The Questionnaire Challenge

The underwriters' counsel will craft a questionnaire for the officers and directors, a "D&O Questionnaire," which is like a detailed self-portrait of their roles and remuneration. The issuer's counsel will be their guides in completing this quest.

(g) The Veracity Check

The lawyers will then embark on a verification voyage, ensuring that all information is consistent and accurate, with no untruths or gaps. This might even involve background checks by private investigators, making sure everyone's story adds up.

(h) The Comprehensive Scrutiny

The underwriters are thorough in their due diligence, driven by their desire to avoid liability. The Securities Act holds them accountable for any material misstatements or omissions, but it also provides them with a "due diligence defense" if they've conducted a reasonable investigation.

(i) The Sarbanes-Oxley Spotlight

Since the Sarbanes-Oxley legislation, the spotlight on due diligence has grown brighter, with a focus on internal controls, financial reporting, and a company's integrity. The underwriters will look for a culture of honesty and compliance, not one of shortcuts and fuzzy accounting.

(j) The Final Review

Just before the final prospectus is prepared, the advisory team will gather for a "bring-down" due diligence, a last-minute check on recent developments. It's a final chance to ask questions and shore up the due diligence defenses.

In essence, due diligence is the great reveal, a process that shines a light on the company's operations, ensuring that what meets the investors' eyes is as honest and accurate as it can be. It's a playful probe into the company's soul, making sure that what lies within is as solid and sparkling as the prospectus promises.

2.12 The SEC's Role in the IPO Drama: A Play by Play

Imagine the SEC as the master of ceremonies at the grand ball of an IPO. Once the registration statement is polished to perfection, it's sent off electronically to the SEC, the ultimate host of this financial gala. The SEC then directs the registration to the fitting industry-related division within its

Division of Corporation Finance, where an examiner and staff accountant are appointed as the company's personal ushers for the event.

(a) The Intermission: SEC's First Review

After the registration statement is filed, there's a brief intermission while the SEC conducts its initial review. Picture this as the moment before the curtain rises, a time of anticipation and final preparations. Typically, within 30 to 35 days, the SEC sends a "comment letter"—like a note from the director with suggestions for a more compelling performance.

(b) The SEC's Spotlight: Adequate Disclosure

The SEC's primary role is to ensure that the prospectus is a transparent window into the company, providing an adequate disclosure of all material facts. Even with a team of seasoned professionals, the art of drafting a prospectus is subjective, and the SEC's comments often seek further clarification or additional information.

(c) Amendments and Adjustments

The company's responses are submitted through amendments to the registration statement, accompanied by a letter from the company's counsel, detailing the changes and any extra information the SEC requested. If the company disagrees with the SEC's direction, a meeting can be requested to discuss the comments and explore possible resolutions.

(d) The iterative Dance of Comment Letters

After the first amendment and response, the company can expect at least one more comment letter from the SEC. It's a dance of refinement, with the SEC and the company going back and forth until the SEC is satisfied with the script.

(e) The Red Herring: Preliminary Prospectus

The preliminary prospectus, affectionately known as the "red herring," is a critical document that the company may be eager to share with potential investors. However, timing is everything. If circulated too early, it may need to be amended or recirculated if the SEC's comments introduce significant changes, which could prove costly and delay the show.

(f) The Final Countdown: Acceleration of Effectiveness

Once the SEC is content with all responses, the company can request to accelerate the effectiveness of the registration statement. With a 48-hour notice, the SEC can declare the registration statement effective, and with all other registrations and applications in place, the curtain can rise, and the company can begin selling to the general public.

Capitalizing on Dreams: Guide to U.S. IPO & Listings

In essence, the SEC's involvement is the critical final act before the company takes center stage. Their guidance ensures that the company's story is told with clarity and honesty, setting the stage for a successful and compliant IPO performance.

2.13 A Garden of Opportunities: The "Emerging Growth Company" and the JOBS Act

Picture the "Emerging Growth Company" (EGC) as a sprout pushing through the soil, eager to grow in the business world. The JOBS Act, signed into law in April 2012, is like a gardener's toolkit, designed to nurture these young companies and reduce the heavy lifting of IPO costs and risks. EGCs are typically small to medium-sized companies with gross annual revenue of less than $1.07 billion in their most recently completed fiscal year.

The JOBS Act, further nurtured by the FAST Act in 2016, is the sun and rain for EGCs, providing a fertile environment for their IPO process. Let's explore the garden of benefits this act offers:

(a) Confidentiality in the Greenhouse

EGCs can now submit draft IPO registration statements to the SEC for a private, behind-the-scenes review. It's like giving the sprout a safe space to grow before it faces the public eye. All drafts are opened to the public at least 15 days before the IPO roadshow begins, or 15 days before the registration statement takes effect if no roadshow is planned.

(b) Testing the Waters

The JOBS Act allows EGCs to have conversations with certain institutional investors to gauge interest in their potential offering. It's like checking the temperature of the water before jumping in.

(c) Reduced Disclosure Requirements

The Act lightens the load by requiring only two years of audited financial statements instead of the usual three. It trims executive compensation disclosures and permits the initial omission of certain financial information, as long as it's properly added before the preliminary prospectus reaches investors. Plus, EGCs can delay complying with new or revised accounting standards that haven't touched private companies yet.

(d) Investment Banks as Gardeners

Investment banks can publish or distribute research reports about an EGC without turning those reports into a formal offer under the Securities Act. It's like getting expert advice on how to best care for the plant.

(e) Phased Growth

Newly public EGCs can gradually adopt post-IPO disclosure requirements over five years. This includes auditor attestations of internal controls, say on pay votes, full executive compensation disclosures, and compliance with new accounting standards. It's like giving the plant time to grow strong stems before bearing the weight of fruit.

In essence, the JOBS Act and the FAST Act are like a gardener's gentle touch, providing the right conditions for EGCs to flourish. With reduced burdens and a supportive environment, these companies can grow from sprouts into the towering trees of the business world.

2.14 Stealth Mode: Filing with the SEC Under the Radar

In the summer of 2017, the SEC's Division of Corporation Finance pulled back the curtain to reveal a new stage for all issuers: the opportunity to submit draft registration statements for IPOs and certain other registrations under a cloak of confidentiality. This was a twist in the play that previously was reserved for only "Emerging Growth Companies" (EGCs) through the JOBS Act and, under specific spotlights, for foreign private issuers.

(a) The Charm of Confidentiality

With this new act, companies can now approach the SEC for a nonpublic review, keeping their offering plans discreet until they're ready to step into the limelight. This is like a secret rehearsal before the big debut, ensuring that the market isn't tipped off until the company is set to take the stage.

(b) Scenarios for a Secret Review

Here are the scenarios where the SEC extends the red carpet for a confidential review:

- **The Debut: Securities Act IPOs and Initial Registrations:** For those on the cusp of their first Securities Act registration statement (think Form S-1 for a traditional IPO, or Form S-11 for REITs), the SEC will take a peek at the draft in private. All the company has to do is promise in a cover letter to go public with the registration statement and the nonpublic drafts at least 15 days before the roadshow begins. If there's no roadshow planned, the reveal should happen 15 days before the registration statement becomes effective.

- **The Exchange Debut: Initial Registration under Exchange Act Section 12(b):** When an issuer is ready to list a class of securities for the first time under Section 12(b) of the Exchange Act (think Form 10 for a spin-off), the SEC will also review drafts confidentially. Again, the issuer must pledge in a cover letter to publicly file the registration statement and drafts 15 days before the anticipated effective date of the registration for the securities listing.

- **The Encore: Securities Act Offerings Post-IPO or Section 12(b) Registration:** If an issuer is planning a Securities Act offering within a year of their IPO or Section 12(b) registration, the SEC will review the draft registration statement on the down-low. The issuer must assure in a cover letter that the registration statement will be publicly available on the EDGAR system at least 48 hours before any requested effective time and date.

(c) **The Grace of Incompleteness** The SEC understands that a draft is just that—a work in progress. So, even if a registration statement isn't fully complete, the SEC won't hold up the review process if the issuer leaves out financial info they believe won't be necessary at the time of the public filing. EGCs have an even greater grace period, as the JOBS Act allows them to omit financial information they reasonably think won't be required at the time of their contemplated offering.

In essence, the SEC's confidential review is like a safe haven for companies preparing to go public, allowing them to keep their plans under wraps until they're ready for the world to see. It's a thoughtful addition to the IPO playbook, giving companies more control over the timing of their public disclosures.

2.15 The Roadshow: A Theatrical Tour of Your Company's

Capitalizing on Dreams: Guide to U.S. IPO & Listings

Story

Once your company has adeptly navigated the SEC's feedback, it's time to don the spotlight and take your narrative to the main stage—the investment community. It's a limited-engagement performance with a strict script, but fear not! The preliminary prospectus is your guide, and the stage is set for a tour de force known as the roadshow.

(a) The Grand Tour: A Whirlwind Adventure

With the preliminary prospectus as your compass, your company's key executives and the managing underwriter will embark on a rapid journey. This is the roadshow—a dynamic series of presentations that span multiple cities over two weeks. Imagine a carefully choreographed dance where the company's vision, competitive edge, distinctive qualities, and financial health take center stage, followed by an interactive Q&A session. This is the heart of the sales pitch; the more intrigue you create, the more enticing your company's perceived value.

(b) Showcasing Your Dream Team

The roadshow is also a showcase for your management team's prowess—leadership, foresight, and trustworthiness. The way you conduct this tour speaks volumes about your company's business ethos.

(c) The Heat is On

In the high-stakes game of capturing investor attention, the roadshow is a pressure cooker. Given its critical role in a successful offering, you might want to enlist the support of a public relations or investor relations firm. Your managing underwriters will also be your trusty sidekicks in this presentation.

(d) The Thrill of the IPO, The Caution of Disclosure

While the excitement of your IPO is palpable, handle with care the information you share during this pre-selling phase. Stick to the script and only discuss what's in the preliminary prospectus. Be vigilant, even in passing chats with friends or family, to avoid letting slip any exclusive news. Keeping company secrets is a must.

(e) The Unscripted Exceptions: Live and Unfiled

Under the SEC's direction, a "live roadshow" is an unwritten dialogue, free from the need to be filed as a free writing prospectus. Slides and other visual aids are exempt from being considered written communications, as long as they are exclusively for the roadshow's eyes and the audience leaves without a copy.

In essence, the roadshow is the crescendo of your IPO journey, where your company's story comes to life for potential investors. It's a carefully planned spectacle that, when executed with finesse, can make all the difference in the success of your public debut.

2.16 The FINRA Finale: Ensuring Compliance for a Curtain Call

As your company prepares for its star turn in the public market, it's crucial to ensure that the underwriting arrangements have not only the SEC's nod but also the seal of approval from FINRA. Think of FINRA as the backstage manager, making sure that everything runs smoothly before the SEC gives the green light for your registration statement to take effect.

(a) The Paper Trail: Documentation for FINRA's Review

To assist FINRA in its review, your company will need to provide a treasure trove of documents detailing the offering and underwriting arrangements. Imagine it as a comprehensive backstage pass, giving FINRA a complete view of the production. Any revisions, amendments, or updates to these documents must be promptly shared with FINRA.

(b) The Web of Relationships: Disclosing Connections

FINRA also demands a spotlight on the relationships between the company, its officers, directors, stockholders, and any FINRA members, including underwriters. This requires a deep dive into the background of stockholders and the transactions between the company and the underwriters. FINRA expects a detailed questionnaire filled out by the company's stockholders, officers, and directors, which should be crafted collaboratively by the underwriter's counsel and company counsel. To keep the show on schedule, this questionnaire should be rolled out early in the process.

(c) Fair Play: Assessing Reasonableness of Fees

At the heart of FINRA's review is the assessment of whether the underwriters' fees are reasonable. According to FINRA's rulebook, no member or associated person should receive compensation that is deemed unfair or unreasonable. The fairness of these fees hinges on the size of the offering, the risks undertaken by the underwriter, the type of securities on offer, and other contextual factors. FINRA will scrutinize the underwriting discount, the commission charged for the IPO, and any items of value that the underwriters or related parties may receive.

(d) The Fine Print: Reviewing Terms for Fairness

FINRA's scrutiny extends to the fine print of the underwriting agreements, sniffing out any unreasonable terms such as excessive reimbursement of expenses or overly favorable rights of first refusal for future offerings. Additionally, FINRA keeps a vigilant eye out for potential conflicts of interest, ensuring that the stage is set for a fair and transparent offering.

In essence, FINRA's role is to ensure that the underwriting arrangements are not just beneficial for the underwriters but also fair for the company and its investors. With thorough documentation, transparent disclosures, and a fair assessment of fees, your company can step into the public market with confidence and credibility.

2.17 The Big Stage: How Your Stock Takes Center Stage on a National Stock Exchange

Imagine your company's stock as a performer ready to take the main stage at the most prestigious theaters of the financial world—the NYSE or NASDAQ. To join the ranks of the traded stars, your company must audition by filing an application and showcasing it meets specific criteria, both financial and governance-wise. It's like ensuring your star has the right balance of talent and professionalism to shine on the big stage.

(a) The Audition Process: Registration and Criteria

The journey begins with registering your stock under the Securities Exchange Act, a bit like acquiring the necessary permits for a public performance. This registration, prepared by company counsel during the IPO process, is filed with the SEC and becomes "effective" at the same time with the company's registration statement under the Securities Act.

(b) Meeting FINRA's Backstage Criteria

Before stepping into the limelight, your company must also meet the FINRA requirements, which we've discussed earlier. It's like getting the final stamps of approval from the backstage crew, ensuring everything from the financial health to the corporate governance is up to snuff.

(c) The Application: Your Ticket to Trading

With all the prerequisites in place, company counsel will craft the application for listing on either the NYSE or NASDAQ. This application is your ticket to the trading floor, where your stock will mingle with the other market players.

(d) The Grand Premiere

Once all the paperwork is in order and the SEC gives its nod, your stock will make its debut on the selected exchange. It's like the curtains opening on a packed house, with all eyes on your company as it begins to trade among the giants of the market.

In essence, getting your stock traded on a national stock exchange is a process of meeting the right criteria, preparing the necessary documents, and ensuring all regulatory boxes are checked. With the right preparation and compliance, your company's stock can take its well-deserved place among the stars of the financial world.

2.18 The Pledge of Commitment: Signing the Underwriting Agreement

Picture the underwriting agreement as the moment when the curtain is about to rise on your company's IPO performance. This crucial document is typically signed after the offering price has been determined and the SEC has given its thumbs-up, declaring the registration statement effective. It's the final handshake before stepping into the spotlight.

(a) The Prelude to Signing

While the fine print and the key terms of the underwriting agreement are hammered out well in advance, the binding commitments don't come into play until the end of the offering process. It's like finalizing the details of a performance right before the audience arrives.

(b) The Safety Net: The Underwriters' "Outs"

Even after the agreement is signed, most underwriting agreements include certain conditions that allow the underwriters to hit the pause button or even terminate the offering if specific events occur. These are known as the underwriters' "outs," and they're like the safety nets that protect the underwriters if the performance doesn't go as planned.

In essence, signing the underwriting agreement is the penultimate step in the IPO journey. It's the official seal of commitment from both parties, signifying that all preparations are complete, and the only thing left to do is to open the curtains and let the offering begin.

2.19 The Underwriters' Reward: A Play on Profit

In the vibrant world of IPOs, underwriters are the maestros who orchestrate the symphony of a public offering. But how do these financial virtuosos earn their melody of earnings?

Contrary to a direct payment from the company, underwriters don't receive a simple salary. Their compensation is more of a performance-based reward, elegantly tied to the success of the offering itself.

In the traditional firm commitment underwriting, underwriters partake in a delightful discount. They secure shares from the company at a price that's a steal compared to what the public will pay—a reduction typically hovering between 4% and 7% off the public offering price.

Think of it as a bulk purchase with an exclusive members' markdown. The underwriters buy in wholesale and then sell to the public at retail. The sweet spot between the purchase price and the selling price? That's the harmonious note of profit that forms the underwriters' payment.

This method is akin to a win-win waltz, where the

underwriters are both the buyers and the sellers, elegantly stepping in and out of roles to ensure the offering's success and their own financial gain.

And let's not forget the little extras—the reimbursement of certain fees—that underwriters may receive, covering the incidental costs of their behind-the-scenes efforts. In essence, the underwriters' payment is a reflection of their pivotal role and the value they add to the IPO's grand performance. It's a payment plan that's as dynamic as the market's rhythm and as rewarding as a standing ovation.

2.20 Unlocking the Payday: When the Shares and Money Change Hands

Imagine the underwriters as eager shoppers at a special sale, and the shares as the prized items they can't wait to get their hands on. But when does the cash register ring, and when do you, as the company, get paid for your stock?

(a) The Closing Curtain: Payment at Closing

The payment for the shares happens at the closing, which is typically scheduled to take place three business days after the pricing of the offering. It's like the final act of a play where all the contracts are signed, and the underwriters hand over the money for the shares they've agreed to purchase.

(b) The Option on the Table: The Over-Allotment Option

In addition to the initial purchase, underwriters are often granted an over-allotment option, colloquially known as the "green shoe" option. This gives them the right to buy extra shares, usually up to 15% more, within a 30-day window. It's like having the option to go back for seconds at a buffet.

(c) Exercising the Option: The Over-Allotment Closing

Should the underwriters decide to exercise this over-allotment option, the additional shares—those "seconds" at the buffet—are purchased at the over-allotment closing. This event typically happens three business days after the underwriters decide to exercise their option.

(d) The Timing Unfolds

So, the payment for the initial shares is made at the closing, and if the over-allotment option is exercised, the payment for those extra shares is made at the subsequent over-allotment closing.

In essence, the payment timeline is neatly packaged into these distinct phases, ensuring a clear and orderly transaction process. It's a well-timed exchange that allows your company to reap the financial benefits of your successful IPO.

2.21 The Consequences of Missteps: Material Misstatements and Omissions in the Registration Statement

Capitalizing on Dreams: Guide to U.S. IPO & Listings

Picture the registration statement as the script of your company's IPO story. What happens if there's a flub in the lines or a scene left out? Let's explore the repercussions of material misstatements or omissions in this all-important document.

(a) The Watchful Eye of Section 11

Section 11 of the Securities Act casts a spotlight on the issuer, its directors, officers who sign the registration statement, underwriters, and any experts named within it. If there's a significant error or something crucial left unsaid, these parties could find themselves in the hot seat. The term "material" refers to information that a reasonable investor would consider important in making a purchase decision.

(b) Proving the Misstep

To prove a misstep, one doesn't need to show intent to deceive, reliance, or negligence. Instead, it's about the presence of a misleading fact or the absence of a necessary one. However, if the defendant can show that the damages weren't caused by the misstatement or omission, no recovery is made.

(c) Affirmative Defenses

There are ways to deflect liability, such as proving the

purchaser knew about the misstatement or omission, although this is often a tough nut to crack in a public offering. For non-issuers, due diligence can serve as a shield, as previously discussed.

(d) Damages and Liability

If a purchaser successfully sues, they're entitled to damages that reflect the difference between the purchase price and the securities' value at the time of the lawsuit. If the securities have been sold, the damages are based on the resale price.

(e) Strict Liability for the Issuer

The issuer is held to strict liability for any material misstatements, meaning no matter the fault or due diligence, they're on the hook. Officers and directors have a due diligence defense at their disposal.

(f) Section 12(a)(2): The Supplemental Clause

Section 12(a)(2) of the Securities Act complements Section 11, focusing on the prospectus or oral communications that may contain untruths or omissions. Liabilities here extend to those who offer or sell securities, including those who actively participate in the solicitation process.

(g) The Broad Reach of Section 12

Unlike Section 11, Section 12(a)(2) includes oral statements made during the public offering, such as those in roadshows and private meetings. It also extends liability to "control persons" unless they can prove ignorance of the facts giving rise to liability.

(h) Rule 159: After-Sale Silencio

Rule 159, adopted by the SEC in 2005, interprets Section 12(a)(2) to exclude any information conveyed to a purchaser after the sale. This underscores the importance of ensuring all material information is shared with the investor before the sale is sealed.

(i) Section 17(a): The Fraud Focus

Section 17(a) of the Securities Act addresses misstatements, misleading statements, and omissions in the IPO registration statement. While courts have held that Section 17(a) doesn't provide a private right of action and is enforceable only by the SEC, it's a reminder of the importance of accuracy in all statements.

(j) Section 15: The Controlling Influence

Section 15 of the Securities Act states that a person controlling another who is liable under the Securities Act may also be held jointly and severally liable. This liability hinges on the controller's knowledge or influence over the misconduct.

For Cooperation, Consultation or Join Group, Please Contact (Tel / WhatsApp / WeChat): +1 (917) 985 7989 (U.S.); +852 5162 6310 (HK); +86 152 1081 6303 (China); Email: CEO@USFinance.Org. If You Also Wish to Publish Your Book(s) Globally, Please Contact Us or Send Us Manuscript(s).

    WhatsApp   WeChat   IPO DreamWorks

CHAPTER THREE

3. CORPORATE HOUSEKEEPING

Preparing for an IPO often involves sprucing up the company's legal and business structure. With changes in securities laws and listing standards, it's crucial to review and adjust corporate governance to ensure compliance post-IPO. This includes addressing "corporate housekeeping" issues to set the stage for a successful public debut.

3.1 The Art of Recapitalization: Setting the Stage for an IPO

As companies prepare to step into the limelight of the stock market, they often engage in a financial facelift known as recapitalization. This strategic move is all about finding the right balance to ensure the company's stock appeals to a broad audience of investors.

(a) Hitting the Right Note: The Target Price Range

The goal is to hit a target price range that resonates with investors. Stocks priced below the $10 mark are often seen as speculative and may not make it onto the shopping lists of some institutional investors who have policies against such purchases. On the flip side, if the price is set too high, it could exclude potential investors by making the purchase of round lots (100 shares) a pricey affair.

(b) The Sweet Spot: Underwriters' Preferred IPO Price

Underwriters typically have a sweet spot in mind for the IPO price: between $10 and $20 per share. This range is enticing for investors and helps ensure a lively trading activity.

(c) Meeting Exchange Requirements: The Price Per Share Floor

National securities exchanges also have their say, setting a minimum price per share and a minimum number of shares for public offerings of listed securities. For many companies, the number of shares they have issued prior to going public might be too few or too many, making the per-share offering price miss the optimal range.

(d) The Recapitalization Toolbox: Stock Splits and More

This is where recapitalization comes into play. With the help of underwriters, companies may decide to adjust the number of outstanding shares to hit that optimal per-share price. This can be done through various means such as a stock split, which increases the number of shares and decreases the price per share, or a reverse stock split, which does the opposite.

(e) Crafting the Perfect Offering: Other Reclassifications

Beyond stock splits, there are other ways to reclassify shares to achieve the desired per-share price. The goal is to create an offering that is not only attractive to investors but also meets the requirements of the exchanges.

In essence, recapitalization is a key step in the pre-IPO process. It's about ensuring that the company's stock is priced right, is in the right quantity, and is poised for success in the public market. It's all about setting the stage for a successful debut and a long-lasting relationship with investors.

3.2 The Grand Conversion: Preferred Securities Before the IPO Curtain Rises

In the corporate world's financial opera, preferred stocks are the lead singers with special solos and privileges. Often, the company's charter is the script that dictates when these stars perform their grand finale, automatically converting into common shares, especially at pivotal moments like an IPO's success.

Issuers may also hold the power to call for this conversion, a strategic bow out from the exclusive rights of preferred securities once the company can stand on its own with IPO capital. This conversion reassures new investors that they won't be overshadowed by the privileges of preferred shareholders.

If automatic conversion isn't set, it's time for some quick backstage deal-making with preferred stockholders to ensure a smooth transition. And if the IPO proceeds with preferred stocks still on stage, Rule 144 acts as a backstage pass, restricting the sale of these shares for a time, easing dilution worries.

In short, converting preferred securities pre-IPO is like a timely plot twist, ensuring a harmonious debut and a smooth performance for all.

3.3 Readying the Stage: Is Your Company's Structure Suited for Public Eyes?

As you prep your company for the IPO limelight, it's crucial to ensure your organizational structure is as clear as a backstage pass. The ideal setup for a business on the cusp of an IPO is a streamlined single corporation or a corporation with well-defined subsidiaries. These structures are like well-rehearsed plays that the investing public can easily follow, with no complex subplots to confuse.

A straightforward structure also shines a light on transparency, making it tough for insider transactions to skulk in the shadows. If your company's organized like a family of affiliated siblings with shared ownership, or if it's woven with partnerships, trusts, or a mix of assorted business entities, it might be time for a structural overhaul.

This transformation can be orchestrated through a series of strategic moves like mergers, re-incorporations, liquidations, or capital contributions. Sometimes, it's about spotlighting the business segment you're keen to present to investors by creating a new corporate entity. Other times, it's about drawing clear lines between existing business lines, perhaps by setting up divisions or subsidiaries.

In essence, aligning your company's structure for an IPO is like rearranging the furniture to make room for new guests. It's about creating a welcoming space that's easy to navigate and understand, setting the stage for a successful public debut.

3.4 Charter Tweaks: Polishing the Corporate Blueprint for the IPO Spotlight

Is your company's charter ready for its close-up? If not, it's time to roll up the sleeves and do some "corporate housekeeping." Tweaking the charter pre-IPO is a wise move, as the hassle and cost of amending it post-IPO can balloon.

(a) The Blueprint Check

During the planning phase, it's crucial to review the charter, all its amendments, and restatements, as well as the bylaws, to ensure they not only comply with the law but also meet the company's needs in the post-IPO era.

(b) Shares for the Future

The charter should allow for a generous pool of authorized capital stock, far exceeding the number of shares issued and outstanding upon completion of the IPO.

This headroom is needed for options, warrants, future offerings, and other potential stock issuances. If the current provisions fall short, it's time to increase the authorized shares. However, be mindful of the tax implications in some states, where the tax bill is tied to the number of authorized shares.

(c) Consider These Charter Amendments

- **Sweep Away the Old**: Remove any provisions that are only relevant to a private company.

- **Open the Doors**: Eliminate any restrictions on the company's structure, duration, or purpose.

- **Preferred Stock Power**: Add provisions for "blank check" preferred stock.

- **Fend Off Unwanted Suitors**: Consider anti-takeover provisions.

- **Board Protection**: Amend the composition, size, and protections of the board of directors.

- **Rebrand if Needed**: A name change might be in order for marketing purposes.

- **Location, Location, Location**: Consider a change in the state of incorporation for more **corporate-**friendly laws.

(d) Streamline the Voting System

Consider eliminating preemptive rights, rights of first refusal, and cumulative voting provisions, if allowed by law. These can complicate the capital structure post-IPO.

In essence, amending the charter is like rearranging the deck chairs on the Titanic—crucial work before the ship sets sail. It's about setting the stage for smooth sailing in the post-IPO waters.

3.5 Bylaws Buff Up: Getting House Rules IPO-Ready

Just as the company's charter is the headline act, the bylaws are the supporting cast that keep the corporate show running smoothly. Preparing for an IPO? It's time to give those bylaws a makeover to match the star's new status.

(a) Mirror, Mirror on the Wall

First up, any changes made to the charter should have their reflection in the bylaws. If the charter's been updated for the IPO stage, the bylaws need their wardrobe change too.

(b) Private to Public Shift

Remember, what worked behind the scenes in a private company might not play well in the public spotlight.

Some bylaws are like old scripts that need new lines to ensure they support the company's governance in its new life as a public entity.

(c) Consider These Bylaw Adjustments

- **The Power to Adapt**: Allow for bylaws to be amended without needing a shareholder's seal of approval.

- **Expand the Board**: Increase the board of directors' size to add more players to the **corporate** governance game.

- **Notice Is Nice**: Specify procedures for advance notice related to shareholder meetings, ensuring everyone's in the loop.

- **Proxy Power**: Enable proxy voting, giving shareholders a voice even when they can't be present.

- **Quorum Call**: Set quorum requirements for shareholder meetings, defining the minimum number of attendees needed for decisions to stick.

(d) The Shareholder Approval Conundrum

While it's tempting to think you can push these changes through without a round of applause from the shareholders, it's generally a good practice to put a restated version of the bylaws up for shareholder ratification. This way, everyone's on board with the new rules of engagement.

In essence, amending the bylaws is like a backstage pass to ensure that the corporate governance structure is not only ready for the IPO but also primed for the company's future success. It's about setting the stage for a smooth transition from private to public and making sure everyone's on the same page.

3.6 Leading the IPO Parade: Management's Key Duties in the Planning and Prep Phases

As the IPO process marches forward like a grand parade, the company's top management is the drum major, leading the way with dedication and commitment. Here's the beat they need to keep:

(a) Time to Shine: Commitment and Dedication

The company's CEO and top brass must be ready to don their top hats and commit the time and energy required to steer the company through the IPO and into its life as a public entity.

(b) Assembling the Dream Team

A key role for the CEO and other advisors is to assemble a team of experts who will become the parade's floats—

experts like underwriters, lawyers, and accountants. They'll make crucial decisions based on the rhythm and input of this team throughout the process.

(c) Tackling the To-Do List: Corporate Housekeeping

In preparation for the public stage, executives should address the "corporate housekeeping" tasks, like cleaning up legal issues and aligning the company's structure for public scrutiny.

(d) Spreading the Word: Communication and Relations

It's also time to consider setting up corporate communication policies and establishing investor and public relations programs to ensure the company's story is well-told and well-received.

(e) The Great Divide: Balancing Acts

With so many IPO responsibilities, there's a risk that the usual management duties may get overshadowed. To prevent the company's operations from missing a beat, it's vital that senior management curates a team of trusted and competent "lieutenants." These are the folks who will ensure the company's day-to-day business keeps humming along while the top brass is preoccupied with the IPO fanfare.

In essence, the management's role in the IPO process is like conducting an orchestra—they must ensure every instrument plays its part perfectly, even as they prepare for their own solo. It's about balancing the preparation for the IPO with the ongoing success of the business.

3.7 Polishing the Corporate Crown: Governance Touch-Ups Before the IPO Curtain

As the company preps for its IPO debut, it's time to make sure the corporate governance tiara is polished to perfection. Here's what needs a final shine:

(a) SEC and Exchange Standards Compliance

The company must team up with its legal dream team to ensure it's ready to dance to the SEC's governance tune, as well as the beat set by the NYSE or NASDAQ. Once the Sarbanes-Oxley Act swings into effect with the filing of the registration statement, it's time to step up to the plate.

(b) Sarbanes-Oxley Symphony

Private companies will find themselves waltzing to the Sarbanes-Oxley tune once they file for an IPO. And for those listing on the NYSE or NASDAQ, there's a gradual groove to get into compliance with board and committee independence requirements. This could start with one independent board member at listing time, a majority within 90 days, and a fully independent board and committees within a year.

(c) The Ideal Compliance Timeline

However, the ideal is to be compliance-ready before the IPO spotlight hits, regardless of the effective dates of the listing requirements. Post-IPO changes could be more of a time- and cost-monster, and the IPO price could take a hit if the company doesn't show it's ready to play by Sarbanes-Oxley and listing standard rules.

(d) Areas of Focus

The following areas are some of the governance gems affected by Sarbanes-Oxley, SEC rulemaking, or the listing standards of the NASDAQ and NYSE:

- **Financial Reporting**: Making sure the numbers tell the right story.

- **Audit Committees**: Assembling a team of financial watchdogs.

- **Executive Compensation**: Balancing the carrot and the stick.

- **Disclosure Practices**: Keeping the company's narrative transparent and engaging.

- **Internal Controls**: Ensuring the company's

operations run like a well-oiled machine.

In essence, addressing corporate governance concerns before going public is like ensuring the stage is set for a flawless performance. It's about showing investors that the company is not just ready for the IPO, but also for the 持续 success that follows in the public eye.

3.8 Setting the Stage for Independence: The Role of Independent Directors

In the world of public companies, the stage is set by rules and regulations from the SEC, NYSE, and NASDAQ, which call for a strong ensemble of independent directors to make up at least a majority of the board. But like any good drama, there's an exception to the rule.

(a) The Controlled Company Exemption

At the NYSE, controlled companies—those with more than 50% of the voting power in the hands of an individual, group, or another company—get a pass on the independence rule. It's like the star actor who's given a bit of leeway because they're the main draw.

(b) Defining "Independence"

But what does "independent" mean in this context? According to the NASDAQ and NYSE, it's a narrow definition that sidesteps any employment, family, or business relationships, as well as compensation committee interlocks, that could cast a shadow on a director's ability to make unbiased decisions.

(c) The True Test of Independence

Independence, in this sense, is like a purity test for directors. They need to be free from any relationship or transaction that could compromise their ability to exercise sound judgment in fulfilling their duties to the company. It's about ensuring that the board's decisions are made with the company's best interests at heart, without any off-stage influences.

In essence, while the majority of a public company's board should be independent, there's some flexibility for controlled companies. But for all others, the focus is on maintaining a board that's as unbiased and impartial as possible, ensuring the company's decisions are made with integrity and transparency.

3.9 The Essential Cast of Committees: Crafting the Board's Supporting Roles

In the orchestrated performance of a public company's governance, the board of directors is the lead ensemble, and its committees are the supporting acts. To harmonize with SEC rules and the NYSE and NASDAQ listing standards, the board must establish several key committees, each with a distinct script:

(a) The Audit Committee: The Financial Guardians

The audit committee is the financial conscience of the company, composed entirely of independent directors. With a minimum of three members, all must meet stringent financial literacy requirements. This committee's functions and responsibilities are to oversee the company's financial health and reporting accuracy. It reviews auditor independence, manages the auditor relationship, and ensures financial statements are a fair and balanced reflection of the company's state. The SEC, NASDAQ, and NYSE have crafted extensive rules for the composition and operation of audit committees.

(b) The Compensation Committee: The Performance Appraisers

As the spotlight shines on executive compensation, the compensation committee takes center stage. This committee is tasked with evaluating and determining the pay for the company's top performers. It must be independent and unbiased, ensuring that executive pay is aligned with company performance and shareholder interests. The committee is also responsible for the annual proxy statement's compensation report, establishing performance-based pay systems, and promoting long-term shareholder value.

(c) The Nominating/Corporate Governance Committee:

The Gatekeepers

The nominating/corporate governance committee is charged with shaping the board's composition and upholding the company's governance standards. It identifies potential director nominees, develops governance principles, reviews director performance, and ensures the board has the right mix of expertise. This committee, too, should be composed of independent directors, guiding the board's structure and practices.

(d) Controlled Company Exceptions: The Special Considerations

For controlled companies, the NYSE offers some exemptions from these requirements. They may not be required to establish a compensation committee or a nominating/corporate governance committee, or to staff these committees solely with independent directors. However, most controlled companies choose to follow the independent model, recognizing its value in maintaining strong governance practices.

In essence, these committees are the board's support system, each playing a critical role in the company's governance, from financial oversight to executive pay to board composition and practices. They ensure that the company's operations are transparent, accountable, and aligned with the best interests of all shareholders.

3.10 Embracing the Script of Ethics: Crafting a Code for Company Leaders

In the world of public companies, the Sarbanes-Oxley Act plays the role of a seasoned director, setting the stage for a critical performance: the adoption of a code of ethics. This code is not just a nice-to-have prop but a mandatory scene for any company stepping into the public eye.

(a) The SEC's Call for Ethics

The SEC has made it clear that all public companies must disclose whether they've adopted a code of ethics for their senior financial officers, including the principal executive officer (CEO), principal financial officer (CFO), principal accounting officer, or controller, or anyone playing similar roles. If a company hasn't adopted such a code, they must provide a clear explanation.

(b) The Blueprint for an Ethical Code

An ethical code that meets the SEC's standards is like a well-written script, designed to deter wrongdoing and promote:

- Honesty and ethical conduct, especially in managing conflicts of interest.

- Transparent and understandable disclosures in SEC filings and public communications.

- Compliance with government laws, rules, and regulations.

- Prompt internal reporting of code violations.

- Accountability for adhering to the code.

(c) Custom Codes for Different Roles

A company can have different codes of ethics tailored to various types of officers. Moreover, these ethical guidelines can be part of a broader code that covers additional topics and applies to more individuals within the company.

(d) Sharing the Code with the Audience

The code of ethics must be made public, either by being exhibited in the Form 10-K or by starring on the company's website. If the website is the stage for the code, the address must be disclosed in the Form 10-K, along with a notice that the code is available there.

(e) Amendments and Waivers in the Spotlight Any changes to the code, or waivers from it, must be disclosed promptly, either in a Form 8-K filed within five business days or on the company's website, provided the website's role in sharing this information has been previously disclosed in the Form 10-K.

In essence, adopting a code of ethics is about setting the right tone for company leadership and ensuring that all actions align with the highest ethical standards. It's a commitment to integrity that resonates with investors, regulators, and the public alike.

3.11 Safeguarding the Guardians: Shielding Directors and Officers from Liability

As a company prepares to take center stage in the public market, it's crucial to ensure that the directors and officers are well-protected from the potential liabilities that come with the spotlight. Here's how to create a shield for these key players:

(a) The Role of Risk Management

With the increased scrutiny that comes from being a public company, directors and officers may face a variety of legal risks, including shareholder suits and third-party claims. To mitigate these risks, companies often provide indemnification and insurance to their management team, which is not only a matter of protection but also a way to attract and retain top talent.

(b) Indemnification: The Legal Safety Net

Indemnification is governed by a mix of state laws and the company's own charter and bylaws. Generally, corporations are required to indemnify directors and officers who win their cases, while those who lose are not indemnified. The statutes give boards broad discretion to set the terms and conditions for indemnification within these boundaries.

(c) The Challenge of Indemnification Post-Scandals

The task of indemnification has become more challenging after financial scandals like Enron and WorldCom shook the market. These events have led to increased caution and restrictions on indemnification coverage.

(d) Directors and Officers Insurance Policies (D&O)

Companies manage their indemnification responsibilities through D&O insurance policies. These policies are essential but can be costly, and they often come with limitations. It's crucial for a company to secure a D&O policy that includes "side A" coverage for directors, providing personal protection for claims not indemnifiable by the corporation.

(e) Assessing the Risks and Policy Options

Before going public, a company should carefully assess its risks and explore all policy options. It's important to review potential policies in detail, considering the financial strength of the underwriters, the definition of covered claims, and the carrier's reputation for handling claims.

(f) SEC Guidelines and Their Impact

The SEC guidelines add another layer of complexity for maintaining D&O insurance. They allow the SEC to share internal investigation reports with the company's D&O carrier, which could potentially lead to policy rescissions if the reports reveal "deliberate fraud." Furthermore, in some cases, the SEC has required officers or directors to forgo indemnification as part of settling cases, adding to the complexity of securing adequate protection.

In essence, protecting directors and officers from liability involves a mix of legal strategies, including indemnification and insurance. It requires careful planning, risk assessment, and policy review to ensure that the company's leaders are safeguarded against the unique challenges they may face in the public domain.

3.12 Navigating the Numbers: Preparing for Accounting Challenges in an IPO

As a company gears up for its IPO debut, it steps into the limelight of financial scrutiny. The SEC's gaze is keen and its focus on the accuracy of financial statements and the practices that underpin them is unyielding. Here's how to make sure those accounting numbers are ready for the big stage:

(a) Early Detection of Accounting Issues

The first act in this financial drama is early detection. Companies and their auditors should play the role of detectives, searching for any potential accounting issues well before the IPO curtains are drawn. The goal is to identify and resolve these issues in the preparatory stages to avoid last-minute surprises that could delay or even derail the IPO.

(b) The Importance of Auditing Practices

The SEC isn't just interested in the numbers; it also examines the auditing and reporting practices that produce those numbers. Companies need to ensure that their financial reporting is transparent, accurate, and in line with Generally Accepted Accounting Principles (GAAP) or International Financial Reporting Standards (IFRS), depending on the requirement.

(c) 3. Pre-Filing Conference with the SEC

When faced with particularly complex accounting issues, it may be wise to request a pre-filing conference with the SEC. This is akin to a rehearsal with the director before the main performance, allowing the company to discuss and resolve potential issues under the SEC's guidance.

(d) Expert Guidance

Given the complexity of accounting standards and the SEC's expectations, it's often beneficial to engage accounting experts who specialize in IPOs. These experts can provide valuable insights and help navigate the intricacies of financial reporting.

(e) Continuous Communication

Maintain open and continuous communication with the SEC throughout the IPO process. This ongoing dialogue can help address questions and clarify expectations, ensuring that the company's financial disclosures meet the SEC's standards.

(f) Investor Relations

Remember, the audience for this financial performance isn't just the SEC; it's also potential investors. Clear and understandable financial disclosures can help build investor confidence and interest in the IPO.

In essence, preparing for accounting issues in an IPO is about thoroughness, transparency, and proactive engagement with the SEC. By addressing accounting challenges head-on and leveraging expert advice, a company can help ensure a smoother journey towards its public debut.

3.13 Choosing the Right Auditor for Your IPO Journey

Capitalizing on Dreams: Guide to U.S. IPO & Listings

When it comes to selecting an auditor for your IPO, it's not just about who you've worked with before—it's about who can best vouch for your financial integrity on the big stage. Here's what you need to keep in mind:

(a) Registered Public Accounting Firm:

Ensure your auditor is registered with the PCAOB (Public Company Accounting Oversight Board) to meet SEC requirements.

(b) National Accounting Firms:

Consider hiring a well-known national accounting firm if you haven't already. Their reputation and expertise can add a layer of trustworthiness to your financial disclosures.

(c) Historical Audits:

If your financial statements lack the national audit stamp of approval, it's wise to have the last three to five years' statements audited by a reputable national firm. This practice can provide a solid foundation for your IPO narrative.

(d) SEC and Regulation S-X Know-How:

National firms come equipped with deep knowledge of SEC procedures and Regulation S-X requirements, which are crucial for your financial reporting and disclosures.

(e) Comfort Letters and Controls:

These firms are also adept at preparing comfort letters and helping you establish robust financial controls, adding to the credibility of your offering.

(f) Early Planning:

Since the audit process can be time-consuming, it's vital to address these considerations early in your IPO planning phase.

In essence, selecting the right auditor is like choosing a reliable co-star for your IPO performance. It's about finding a partner who not only understands the rules but also brings a track record of successful collaborations to the table.

3.14 Auditor Eligibility Under Sarbanes-Oxley: A Checklist for Compliance

Before your company embarks on the IPO journey, ensuring the eligibility of your current or prospective accounting firm under Sarbanes-Oxley is crucial. Here's a concise guide to help you navigate this important aspect:

(a) Auditor Independence:

Confirm that your accounting firm is independent and

doesn't have any relationships that could compromise this status.

(b) SEC Rules:

The SEC has established extensive rules on auditor independence. Make sure your firm is aware of and compliant with these regulations.

(c) Disclosure of Fees:

Be prepared to disclose the fees billed by the auditor for both audit and non-audit services. Transparency in fee structures is key.

(d) Prohibition of Certain Services:

Certain non-audit services are prohibited under Sarbanes-Oxley. Ensure your firm does not provide any services that could be considered a violation.

(e) Billing Ratio Concerns:

A significant billing for non-audit services compared to audit services can raise red flags with the SEC and investors. Keep this ratio in check to avoid any potential issues.

(f) Partner Rotation Rule:

The SEC mandates that lead and concurring partners from the accounting firm cannot provide audit services for more than five consecutive years. This includes time when the company was private.

By keeping these points in mind, you can help ensure that your accounting firm is eligible to audit your financial statements under Sarbanes-Oxley, setting a solid foundation for your IPO process.

3.15 Spotlight on IPO Accounting: Navigating Key Concerns

As your company gears up for an IPO, the stage is set for intense accounting scrutiny. Here are the key accounting issues to watch:

(a) Auditor Review:

Post-selection, the auditor must meticulously review the company's accounting policies, practices, and internal financial controls. This includes a deep dive into acquisitions, mergers, pro forma statements, and past management letters.

(b) Segment Reporting and Revenue Recognition:

The auditor should assess if segment reporting applies and if the company's revenue recognition aligns with industry peers.

(c) Income Statement Classifications:

The SEC pays close attention to how items are classified in the income statement, so the auditor must review these classifications with care.

(d) Transition from Private to Public Practices:

The auditor should evaluate the company's accounting principles and practices as a private entity to ensure they transition smoothly to public standards.

(e) Internal Control Deficiencies:

Any significant weaknesses in financial reporting controls must be addressed promptly.

(f) The "Cheap Stock" Issue:

If stock or options were granted at prices below fair market value, especially if the IPO price significantly exceeds these, the SEC may require recording the difference as unearned compensation or sales expense, impacting earnings and potentially necessitating financial statement restatements.

(g) SEC Scrutiny on Grants:

Stock or option grants made close to the IPO, typically within one to two years prior, may attract SEC attention.

It's crucial to establish fair market value, ideally through an independent appraisal, and consult with auditors during the grant process and financial reporting.

(h) Proactive Defense:

Be prepared to justify past stock and option pricing to the SEC to avoid IPO disruptions or delays.

(i) Reorganization and Recapitalization:

Complex accounting issues may arise from pre-IPO reorganizations or recapitalizations. Engaging auditors early in these processes can help anticipate and address the impact on financial statements.

By proactively addressing these accounting issues with the guidance of your auditor, you can help ensure a smoother path to your public market debut.

3.16 Fortifying the Bulwarks: Preparing for Takeover Defenses in an IPO

As your company stands on the brink of going public, it's worth considering whether to shore up defenses against future takeover attempts that might not align with shareholder interests. Here's a concise overview:

(a) Pre-IPO Planning:

It's advisable to evaluate the need for anti-takeover measures before, not after, the IPO due to investor perceptions and the complexities of amending the charter post-IPO.

(b) Investor Relations:

The public often views anti-takeover measures as entrenchment strategies that could diminish shareholder value.

(c) Charter Amendments:

Post-IPO, obtaining shareholder approval for charter amendments that introduce anti-takeover measures can be challenging, time-consuming, and costly.

(d) Consultation with IPO Team:

Engage with your IPO advisors, especially legal counsel and underwriters, to discuss the adoption of anti-takeover measures.

(e) Legal Compliance:

Ensure any anti-takeover measures comply with state corporate laws and are clearly disclosed in the registration statement.

(f) Impact on IPO Valuation:

Consider the potential impact of such measures on the per-share IPO price, as they could affect investor interest and valuation.

(g) Institutional Shareholder Resistance:

Be aware that institutional shareholders and activist investors often oppose anti-takeover measures.

(h) Underwriter Guidance:

Some underwriters may advise against adopting anti-takeover provisions due to their perceived impact on IPO marketing and pricing.

(i) State Law Protections:

Consider state law provisions that offer shareholder protections, such as non-shareholder constituency provisions, control share acquisition, and business combination rules.

(j) Staggered Board:

A staggered board can prevent immediate takeover through director elections.

(k) Director Removal:

Charter provisions may allow for director removal only for cause, protecting the board composition.

(l) Supermajority Voting:

Requiring a supermajority vote for certain corporate actions can strengthen anti-takeover defenses.

(m) Meeting and Consent Provisions:

Removing shareholder rights to call special meetings or act by written consent can limit proxy contest opportunities.

(n) Director Number and Vacancies:

Limiting the shareholder ability to change the board size or fill vacancies can protect against hostile takeovers.

(o) Shareholder Proposals and Nominations:

Establishing advance notice requirements for shareholder proposals or director nominations can provide a layer of defense.

(p) Poison Pill:

Shareholder rights plans, or poison pills, can deter hostile takeovers by granting shareholders the right to buy additional stock at a discount under certain conditions.

(q) Activist Shareholder Pressure:

Be prepared for pressure from activist shareholders and proxy advisory services to dismantle takeover defenses.

(r) Proxy Advisory Services:

Services like ISS can influence institutional shareholders' voting behavior and may oppose certain anti-takeover measures.

(s) Weighing the Pros and Cons:

Carefully consider the advantages and disadvantages of adopting anti-takeover measures with the guidance of legal counsel.

By taking these considerations into account, your company can make informed decisions about the best way to protect its interests and those of its shareholders in the face of potential takeover attempts.

3.17 Aligning Employment Agreements with Public Standards: A Pre-IPO Checklist

As your company preps for its public debut, it's vital to ensure that employment agreements are in tune with public company norms. Here's a concise guide to evaluating and adjusting these agreements:

(a) Disclosure Requirements:

Remember, the terms of significant employment agreements must be disclosed in the registration statement, so they should be structured to meet public market expectations.

(b) Market Perception of Reasonableness:

Scrutinize the terms, especially compensation packages, to ensure they will be perceived as reasonable by the market. Overly generous deals may raise eyebrows among potential investors.

(c) Re-negotiation of Lucrative Agreements:

If employment contracts with major shareholders are excessively beneficial, consider re-negotiating them to align with public company standards and investor expectations.

(d) Employee Loyalty and Retention:

If key employees lack employment contracts, it might be wise to negotiate such agreements to foster loyalty and retention, which are crucial for the company's ongoing success.

(e) Severance Protection for Management:

Post-IPO, the board and senior management may lose some control. It's worth considering whether severance protection is appropriate for these individuals, given their role in the company's future.

(f) Alignment with Corporate Strategy:

Ensure that employment agreements support the company's strategic goals and do not hinder its flexibility or growth plans.

(g) Legal Compliance:

Verify that all agreements comply with applicable laws and regulations, including those related to employment, labor, and taxation.

(h) Consultation with Advisors:

Work closely with legal and HR advisors to review and revise employment agreements, ensuring they are appropriate for a public company.

By carefully reviewing and adjusting employment agreements pre-IPO, your company can set the stage for a successful transition to public life, attracting and retaining top talent while maintaining investor confidence.

3.18 Refining the Employee Benefit Plan for an IPO: A

Capitalizing on Dreams: Guide to U.S. IPO & Listings

Strategic **Overview**

As your company contemplates an IPO, it's a prime time to evaluate and refine the employee benefit plan, particularly if it includes stock options. Here's a concise breakdown of the key considerations:

(i) Incentive Alignment: Assess whether the plan effectively incentivizes employees, aligning their interests with the company's long-term growth and success.

(j) Share Allocation:

Ensure the plan allocates a sufficient number of shares for future grants. Avoid being overly generous to prevent a potentially negative impact on the market, known as "overhang."

(k) Regulatory Compliance:

Confirm that the plan meets the latest securities law requirements, especially those related to Section 16's short-swing trading rules, which can affect how quickly and under what conditions shares acquired through the plan can be traded.

(l) Simplicity of Amendment:

Recognize that amending a plan is more straightforward while the company is private. Post-IPO, obtaining stockholder approval can be more complex and time-consuming.

(m) Market Perception:

Consider how the benefit plan, including any stock options, will be perceived by the market and investors. The plan should strike a balance between attracting talent and not diluting investor confidence.

(n) Financial Implications:

Evaluate the financial impact of the plan on the company, including the potential dilution of shares and the accounting treatment of stock options.

(o) Advisory Support:

Consult with legal, HR, and financial advisors to help assess the current plan and draft any necessary amendments or new plans.

(p) Timing:

If amendments are needed, it's best to address them pre-IPO to avoid complications and additional costs associated with changes post-IPO.

By proactively reviewing and adjusting the employee benefit plan, your company can ensure it supports both employee engagement and shareholder value as you transition to the public markets.

3.19 Equipping for Success: Crafting New Equity Compensation Plans Pre-IPO

As your company eyes the horizon of an Initial Public Offering (IPO), it's a strategic moment to consider new equity compensation plans. These plans can be instrumental in retaining talent, offering flexible reward structures, and compensating non-employee directors. Here's a snapshot of the key plans to contemplate:

(a) Employee Stock Purchase Plan (ESPP):

An ESPP allows employees to buy company stock at a slight discount to its market value, often with tax advantages. This can be a powerful tool for retention, particularly if the stock price appreciates post-IPO.

(b) "Omnibus" Plan:

This comprehensive plan offers a suite of benefits including restricted stock, bonus stock awards, and stock appreciation rights (SARs). It provides management with the flexibility to tailor compensation packages to the needs of various employees.

When crafting these plans, consider the following:

(c) Retain Talent:

Ensure the plans are structured to effectively retain key employees by aligning their interests with the company's performance.

(d) Flexibility in Awards:

The "Omnibus" plan, with its varied options, can be particularly useful for offering a range of compensation awards that can adapt to different roles and contributions.

(e) Compensation for Non-Employee Directors:

If your company intends to compensate non-employee directors with equity, an "Omnibus" plan can provide a framework for such awards.

(f) Accounting Implications:

Be mindful of the recent changes in accounting rules for stock-based compensation. The nature of equity awards and the chosen plans should be designed to comply with these regulations.

(g) Market Perception:

Consider how new equity plans will be perceived by the market and investors. Transparency and the alignment of these plans with shareholder interests are crucial.

(h) Legal and Financial Advisory:

Work closely with legal and financial advisors to structure the plans to meet the company's objectives while considering tax implications and regulatory requirements.

By thoughtfully designing and implementing new equity compensation plans, your company can enhance its attractiveness to employees and directors, fostering a culture of ownership and commitment that can contribute to the success of your IPO and beyond.

3.20 Shareholder Nods for Equity Plans

Aye, Shareholders Aboard!

The NYSE and NASDAQ have set the sails: material changes to equity compensation plans need the approval of your shareholders. Most exceptions have been cast away, but a few 'grandfathered' ones may still float around. Scrutinize your unapproved plans to spot any.

Crafting new or tweaking existing plans? Call upon your legal team to navigate the new executive compensation waters.

For Cooperation, Consultation or Join Group, Please Contact

Capitalizing on Dreams: Guide to U.S. IPO & Listings

(Tel / WhatsApp / WeChat): +1 (917) 985 7989 (U.S.); +852 5162 6310 (HK); +86 152 1081 6303 (China); Email: CEO@USFinance.Org. If You Also Wish to Publish Your Book(s) Globally, Please Contact Us or Send Us Manuscript(s).

WhatsApp   WeChat   IPO DreamWorks

CHAPTER FOUR

4. The Art of Public Communication During the IPO Registration Process

Silent IPO Seas

During the IPO voyage, federal securities laws quietly impose restrictions on public communication. Keep these in mind as you steer your message to the world.

Bon Voyage!

Stay on course with compliance and transparency, and may your corporate journey be smooth sailing!

4.1 Navigating the Quiet Seas: Understanding Gun-Jumping

In the intricate dance of federal securities laws, the aim is to maintain a delicate balance—limiting pre-offering publicity while allowing issuers to shine their brand. The term "gun-jumping" refers to the act of prematurely stirring the market's waters with information or excitement about an issuer before the SEC's mandated prospectus has been presented to investors. The SEC vigilantly enforces these rules, sometimes requiring a cooling-off period before an IPO can proceed.

(a) The SEC's Liberal Touch in 2005

While the SEC acknowledges the need for issuers to make waves in the marketplace, the 2005 relaxation of communication restrictions mostly favors seasoned companies with follow-on offerings. For those on the brink of an IPO, the communication constraints remain largely in place.

(b) The Three Waves of Communication:

- **The Pre-Filing or "Quiet" Period:** A time of silence before the registration statement is filed, where issuers must tread lightly to avoid any premature disclosures.

- **The Waiting Period:** Once the registration statement is filed but before it becomes effective, issuers are in a holding pattern, where they must wait for the SEC's go-ahead to engage in certain promotional activities.

- **The Post-Effective Period:** After the registration statement is effective, issuers gain more freedom to communicate, though they must still sail within the boundaries set by the SEC.

(c) Staying Afloat with SEC Guidelines

Ensuring that promotional activities align with SEC's acceptable publicity is crucial. Issuers must carefully navigate these periods to avoid the perils of gun-jumping, ensuring a smooth and compliant journey towards a successful IPO.

(d) Bon Voyage to Compliant Communication!

With a keen understanding of the SEC's guidelines and a strategic approach to communication, companies can effectively promote themselves without running afoul of the rules. Keep the message clear, the timing right, and may your voyage to the public markets be smooth sailing!

4.2 The Silent Prelude: Unveiling the "Quiet Period" in Finance

Embark on a thrilling journey into the captivating realm of finance, where we unveil the mystique of the "Quiet Period"! Imagine it as the suspenseful silence before the curtain rises on a grand stage, a secret kept close to the chest until the opportune moment arrives.

Envision this scenario: a company has just secured the tentative interest of an underwriter, akin to a clandestine rendezvous. But, patience is a virtue! Before the world can witness this alliance, there exists a period of hushed anticipation, a 'pre-filing' interlude, where everything remains shrouded in secrecy. This is the essence of the "Quiet Period."

Think of it as the conspiratorial whispers between two parties, plotting their grand strategy in the shadows. It's the interim phase following the tentative agreement and preceding the public filing of the registration statement. It's the serene calm before the storm, the pause that precedes the thunderous applause.

4.3 Whispers in the Wind: Navigating the Communication Boundaries of the Quiet Period

Ah, the enigmatic "Quiet Period," a time when the world of finance holds its breath, waiting for the next big move. But what are the unspoken rules that govern this silent era? Let's delve into the hushed corridors of finance to discover the restrictions imposed on communications during this time.

According to the wise old Section 5(c) of the Securities Act, it's a no-no to offer to sell or buy any security until the registration statement has been filed. This means that the federal securities laws put a firm 'mute' button on any offers until the paperwork is officially in the system. The term "offer" is as broad as the ocean, implying that any pre-filing fanfare could be considered 'gun-jumping' if it's not justified by permissible business purposes.

Now, this might seem a bit draconian for issuers. Imagine a company that's suddenly the center of online gossip—ignoring it could be career suicide, but responding might be seen as jumping the gun. Fortunately, the SEC has a heart and recognizes the need for companies, especially the fresh-faced ones, to stand up and be counted.

Capitalizing on Dreams: Guide to U.S. IPO & Listings

The fine line between sharing facts and soliciting is as delicate as a spider's web, easily crossed, often unintentionally. To help companies navigate these treacherous waters, the SEC has thrown a lifeline in the form of guidelines. These guidelines suggest that issuers can continue to:

(a) Flaunt their products and services in advertisements.

(b) Send out the usual quarterly and annual reports to their shareholders.

(c) Publish proxy statements and dispatch dividend notifications.

(d) Release press releases about the company's business and financial happenings.

(e) Hold regular shareholders' meetings to address inquiries on factual matters.

Additionally, they can respond to unsolicited questions from securities analysts, financial analysts, the media, shareholders, and others. But remember, private companies have a different set of communication needs compared to their public counterparts.

In the digital age, most companies have a virtual storefront in the form of a website, teeming with information. The pre-clearance and posting of information on these sites can be a minefield, especially during the IPO process. Companies must keep a hawk's eye on their websites to ensure that no information, whether it's in the site or linked to it, influences potential investors' decisions about the IPO.

For those setting up websites around the IPO process, timing is everything. It's crucial to discuss these timing issues with legal counsel. During the pre-filing period, it's vital to review all public communications with company counsel before they see the light of day, and to weigh the necessity and justification for any publicity.

So, there you have it—a glimpse into the silent ballet of the Quiet Period, where every move is measured, every word is weighed, and the stage is set for the grand performance to come.

4.4 Leaping Too Soon: The Consequences of SEC's Gun-Jumping

Ah, the perilous dance of timing in the world of finance! What happens if the SEC suspects a company of 'jumping the gun'? Let's explore the possible penalties that could come knocking on the company's door.

Firstly, the SEC might pull out the 'time-out' card, asking the company to press pause on its offering for a few weeks. Or, they could demand that the company spills the beans in the statutory prospectus, disclosing all the details from the impermissible publicity. They might also insist on adding a risk factor, warning that investors have the right to rescind their purchases or claim damages.

These remedies might throw a wrench in the works of an offering, but they're a walk in the park compared to the big bad wolf: a formal enforcement action by the SEC. The SEC staff usually reserves this for the really naughty cases.

Let's take a trip down memory lane to Google's IPO. Before Google could say "I'm feeling lucky," Playboy magazine published an interview with the founders that had taken place months earlier. Since this happened before Google filed its registration statement, the SEC made Google amend its registration statement to include the full text of the Playboy article and iron out some discrepancies.

Similarly, Salesforce.com almost tripped over its own feet. Less than a week before its planned IPO, the CEO gave an interview to the Wall Street Journal. The SEC wasn't amused and ruled that Salesforce.com had violated the gun-jumping rules, delaying the IPO for more than a month.

So, the moral of the story? Patience is a virtue in the world of finance. Jumping the gun might seem like a shortcut, but it could lead to a longer and bumpier road. It's always better to play by the rules and let the good times roll at the right moment.

4.5 Navigating the Quiet Waters: Safe Harbors for Communications in the Pre-Filing Period

Capitalizing on Dreams: Guide to U.S. IPO & Listings

In the hushed silence of the pre-filing period, the SEC has thoughtfully laid out a few 'safe harbors'—think of them as lifeboats—for companies to cling to while navigating the choppy waters of permissible communications.

Let's cast our nets into these safe harbors:

Rule 163A offers a non-exclusive sanctuary for certain communications that are made more than 30 days before the registration statement is filed. To sail into this haven, a company must adhere to these conditions:

- The communication must not allude to the securities offering that is the subject of the registration statement.

- The communication must be made by or on behalf of the issuer, meaning the issuer must give the green light to the Rule 163A communication.

- The issuer must take "reasonable steps within its control" to prevent the information from spreading further during the 30-day period before filing the registration statement.

•

Rule 135 throws a lifeline to companies by stating that a notice of a proposed offering (in the form of a press release or a written communication to security holders or employees) is not considered an "offer to sell" if it meets these criteria:

- The notice clearly states that it does not constitute an offer of any securities for sale.

- The notice contains only very limited information, such as the name of the issuer, the title, amount, and basic terms of the securities offered, the amount to be offered by selling shareholders (if any), the anticipated timing of the offering, and a brief statement regarding the manner and purpose of the offering (without naming the underwriters).

Bear in mind, companies typically don't use a pre-filing notice unless they believe the upcoming offering is a significant development that should be disclosed to investors.

Lastly, **Rule 169** opens the floodgates for a company to release or disseminate factual business information at any time, including before or after the filing of a registration statement, provided these conditions are met:

- The company has previously released or disseminated similar types of information in the ordinary course of its business.

- The timing, manner, and form of the release or dissemination are consistent with past practices.

- The information is intended for use by individuals other than investors or potential investors, and is released by the company's employees or agents who have historically provided such information.

It's important to note that the Rule 169 safe harbor does not apply to forward-looking statements, and the information released must not be related to the offering.

So, with these safe harbors as our guide, companies can steer clear of the rocky shores and sail smoothly through the pre-filing period, ready to embark on the exciting journey ahead.

4.6 The Quiet Before the Storm: The Waiting Period Explained

Think of the "waiting period" as the brief, suspenseful pause right after an IPO registration statement is filed and before the SEC gives it the green light. It's a time when the company and its team fine-tune their strategy, responding to SEC and FINRA comments, prepping for the roadshow, and finalizing underwriting deals.

During this phase, companies can make offers for their securities but can't actually sell them yet. The rules for making these offers are strictly regulated to keep everything on the up and up.

So, the waiting period isn't just a lull; it's a crucial phase of preparation, setting the stage for the exciting debut on the market's stage.

4.7 The Art of Marketing Under Wraps: Restrictions on Written Materials During the Waiting Period

In the quietude of the waiting period, the marketing of a company's stock is carefully choreographed. Prospective investors can be approached through oral presentations and via the preliminary prospectus or free-writing prospectus, but the use of any other written materials is off-limits. The SEC casts a wide net when defining what constitutes an "offer," sweeping in a broad array of communications, from traditional print ads to digital media, emails, and even audio and video content.

It's crucial to remember that during this period, broadcasting offers via radio, TV, or recordings is strictly verboten. Live presentations, such as those using slides or PowerPoint, are considered oral communications as long as they're not distributed, sidestepping the need for filing and other regulatory requirements.

Post-registration statement filing, when a price range is set, companies and their partners can unleash "free-writing prospectuses" onto the scene. These are offers to sell in written form that aren't bound by the same rules as statutory prospectuses. They can take any shape or form and must carry a specific legend. Typically, they need to be filed with the SEC before their first use, and they should be accompanied by the most recent statutory prospectus, often in an electronic format with a direct link.

Importantly, free-writing prospectuses must harmonize with the registration statement and are subject to a three-year retention period by the issuer or those using them in the offering.

Despite these guidelines, underwriters often craft internal sales documents for their sales force's eyes only. These documents are strictly confidential and are not to be shared with or presented to potential stock purchasers in the IPO.

4.8 The Fine Art of Verbal Pitching: Navigating Oral Marketing Restrictions During the Waiting Period

Once the registration statement is filed, the stage is set for oral marketing of a company's stock. However, the script for these verbal exchanges must stick to the narrative laid out in the preliminary prospectus. Straying from this script by offering additional details to certain investors could lead to a scenario the SEC dubs "selective disclosure," which is a game no one wants to play.

Expanding on topics from the prospectus is common during oral communications, but issuers must avoid revealing material information that hasn't made it to the prospectus, such as secret sauce financial projections.

The quintessential oral communication event is the roadshow, typically a live, in-person performance for a select audience. These presentations are exempt from SEC filing requirements. But if a roadshow isn't a live, real-time affair, it would usually need to be filed as a free-writing prospectus. To dodge this requirement, companies can make an electronic version of the roadshow accessible to all potential investors.

The 1999 IPO of Webvan Group Inc. serves as a cautionary tale. During their roadshow, the financial media caught wind of undisclosed information that wasn't part of the preliminary prospectus. The SEC stepped in, demanding Webvan to update their registration statement with this new data, redistribute the revised prospectus to investors, and cool their heels through a mandated waiting period before they could proceed with going public.

So, the moral of the story? Keep your oral marketing on-message and in sync with the preliminary prospectus to avoid an unexpected plot twist with the SEC.

4.9 Steering Clear of Spotlights: General Publicity During the Waiting Period

During the waiting period, the rules of engagement for marketing an IPO extend beyond the company's direct communications, affecting its broader advertising and publicity strategies. This phase is even more sensitive than the period preceding the initial filing of the registration statement. Any uptick in advertising and publicity, regardless of the target audience, can trigger scrutiny, especially if it's perceived to be part of an IPO push.

Engagements like interviews with senior executives,

conference appearances, and trade show speeches could all potentially raise red flags. It's imperative that any publicity involving the company or its top brass be vetted by the company's legal counsel before moving forward. The same prudence applied to the company's website during the pre-filing period should continue through the waiting period.

While it's impossible to control every narrative third parties might spin about the company, caution is key when cooperating with them. Any assistance provided could inadvertently position the company as the "source" of the story, which could lead to complications.

When contemplating publicity, whether before filing or during the waiting period, remember that the best intentions can sometimes be misconstrued by the SEC or even investors post-IPO. Since preemptive consultation with these parties isn't feasible, it's wise to adopt a cautious approach to avoid any missteps that could cast a shadow over the company's IPO journey.

4.10 Crafting the Cryptic Call: Designing a "Tombstone Ad" Amidst the Waiting Period

In the shadow of the waiting period, Rule 134 casts a light on the creation of "tombstone" ads, offering a skeletal framework for permissible disclosures about an IPO. Here's what you can include in these cryptic communications:

- The essentials from a Rule 135 release.

- A succinct, unembellished depiction of the issuer's business sector.

- The price of the securities or, if elusive, the method for determining it or a rough price range as indicated by the issuer or the managing underwriters.

- The managing underwriters' names.

- An approximate date for the public sale's commencement.

- A smattering of other pertinent details specific to the company or security on offer.

The SEC keeps a hawk-eyed vigil on Rule 134, demanding a business description as plain as day, devoid of adjectives or speculative forecasts. Phrases like "leading provider" or "expected to expand into" are best left unsaid.

Should a company opt for a tombstone ad under Rule 134, it must also weave in certain mandatory elements:

- The intended use of the offering proceeds.

- A legend clarifying that the registration statement is pending effectiveness, no offers are yet acceptable, and the ad itself isn't an offer.

- Contact details for obtaining a preliminary prospectus.

The stakes are high for compliance with Rule 134; non-compliance could lead the SEC to insist on a risk factor in the prospectus, hinting at buyer rescission rights due to a potential Section 5 violation.

In essence, tombstone ads are the cryptic whispers of the financial world, carefully crafted to respect the SEC's rules while quietly announcing an impending offering.

4.11 The Digital Stage: Unveiling the Internet Roadshow

An Internet roadshow is a modern twist on the traditional roadshow, leveraging the power of the web to reach potential investors.

Unlike live, real-time roadshows, which are categorized as oral communications, a prerecorded electronic roadshow is viewed as a written communication. This digital presentation is akin to a free writing prospectus and must carry the mandatory boilerplate legend as stipulated by Rule 433.

For an Initial Public Offering (IPO), the electronic roadshow dodges the requirement to be filed as a free writing prospectus under Rule 433 if the issuer ensures that at least one "bona fide" version of this digital show is freely accessible to all potential investors.

This version, while covering similar ground regarding the issuer, its leadership, and the securities on offer, isn't obliged to mirror every detail or interactive element of other versions.

If the electronic roadshow escapes the filing requirement, any accompanying materials like visual aids or slideshows also slip through the net if they're presented as an integral part of the roadshow.

However, if these materials are distributed separately or appear designed for independent replication by the audience, they're treated as free writing prospectuses.

In essence, an Internet roadshow is a savvy adaptation, allowing companies to showcase their offerings in a prerecorded format while navigating the regulatory landscape with care.

It's a testament to the evolving landscape where technology meets finance, offering a platform that's both accessible and compliant.

4.12 Engaging Digitally: Handling Bulletin Boards and Chat Rooms During the Waiting Period

During the waiting period, companies face challenges in addressing negative comments on online platforms like bulletin boards and chat rooms.

However, the SEC is generally accommodating and allows

companies to respond to such negativity, as long as their responses stay true to the information already presented in the prospectus. This policy helps companies clear the air without overstepping regulatory bounds.

4.13 Safeguarding Against Violations: Precautions During the Registration Period

To navigate the registration period without tripping over regulatory restrictions, consider these streamlined guidelines:

(a) Centralize Media Communications:

Designate a single point of contact for all media inquiries to ensure consistent messaging.

(b) Maintain Business-as-Usual in Promotions:

Keep advertising and publicity aligned with historical practices, focusing on service quality and company reputation.

(c) Avoid Financial Disclosures:

Steer clear of discussing financial conditions, growth rates, projections, or earnings per share.

(d) Target the Right Audience:

Direct promotional efforts towards customers, not

investors, and avoid media heavily used by the investment community.

(e) Skip Industry Gatherings:

Refrain from addressing groups of securities analysts or investment professionals.

(f) No Unsolicited Materials:

Avoid distributing promotional materials to potential investors or professionals unless it's necessary and compliant.

(g) Mute the Offering Mention:

Omit any reference to the public offering in ads and don't offer unsolicited information about it to the media.

(h) Educate on Legal Limitations:

If asked about the offering, clarify the legal restrictions on discussing it.

(i) Comply with Disclosure Laws:

Ensure timely and accurate SEC filings for periodic reporting and be mindful of the continuous disclosure requirement for material information.

(j) Fair Play with Information:

Prevent selective disclosure by sharing material nonpublic information only with those who need to know, and once shared beyond this circle, make it public knowledge promptly.

By adhering to these principles, a company can effectively manage its public image and communications during the registration period while staying within the regulatory framework.

For Cooperation, Consultation or Join Group, Please Contact (Tel / WhatsApp / WeChat): +1 (917) 985 7989 (U.S.); +852 5162 6310 (HK); +86 152 1081 6303 (China); Email: CEO@USFinance.Org. If You Also Wish to Publish Your Book(s) Globally, Please Contact Us or Send Us Manuscript(s).

Capitalizing on Dreams: Guide to U.S. IPO & Listings

WhatsApp   **WeChat**   **IPO DreamWorks**

CHAPTER FIVE

5. On Going Disclosure Obligations and Requirements

5.1 Essential Filings: A Concise Guide to SEC Documents

For a company aspiring to list on the NYSE or NASDAQ, the journey begins with registration under the Securities Exchange Act, setting the stage for a series of critical SEC filings that ensure transparency and regulatory compliance.

(a) Form 8-A:

This form marks the company's initial registration of a class of securities, triggering ongoing periodic disclosure obligations under Section 13(a) of the Securities Exchange Act.

(b) Form 10-K:

An annual report providing a granular view of the company's financial health and operations. It includes:

- Audited balance sheets for the last two fiscal years.

- Audited income statements for the last three years.

- Management's Discussion and Analysis (MD&A) offering insights into financial trends and future uncertainties.

- A report on the effectiveness of internal control over financial reporting, alongside the external auditor's assessment.

- Narrative descriptions of the company's business, properties, management, shareholder information, and more.

- Risk factors and any material changes to them.

- Disclosure of insider noncompliance with Section 16(a) reporting obligations.

- The report must be signed by principal officers and a majority of the board, with specific certifications by the CEO and CFO.

(c) Form 10-Q:

A quarterly report that mirrors some elements of the Form 10-K but on an unaudited basis, covering financial statements, MD&A, and internal control assessments over financial reporting for each quarter.

(d) Form 8-K:

A current report capturing significant corporate events as they occur, such as entering or terminating a material definitive agreement, bankruptcy, changes in control, or significant financial obligations. The specific events are as followed:

Items	Descriptions
1.01	Entry into a Material Definitive Agreement
1.02	Termination of a Material Definitive Agreement
1.03	Bankruptcy or Receivership
1.04	Mine Safety – Reporting of Shutdowns and Patterns of Violations
2.01	Completion of Acquisition of Disposition of Assets
2.02	Results of Operations and Financial Condition
2.03	Creation of a Direct Financial Obligation or an Obligation Under an Off-Balance Sheet Arrangement of a Registrant
2.04	Triggering Events that Accelerate or Increase a Direct Financial Obligation or an Obligation Under an Off-Balance Sheet Arrangement
2.05	Costs Associated with Exit or Disposal Activities
2.06	Material Impairments
3.01	Notice of Delisting or Failure to Satisfy a Continued Listing Rule or Standard; Transfer of Listing
3.02	Unregistered Sales of Equity Securities

Capitalizing on Dreams: Guide to U.S. IPO & Listings

Items	Descriptions
3.03	Material Modifications to Rights of Security Holders
4.01	Changes in Registrant's Certifying Accountant
4.02	Non-Reliance on Previously Issued Financial Statements or a Related Audit Report or Completed Interim Review
5.01	Changes in Control of Registrant
5.02	Departure of Directors or Certain Officers; Election of Directors; Appointment of Certain Officers; Compensatory Arrangements of Certain Officers
5.03	Amendments to Articles of Incorporation or Bylaws; Change in Fiscal Year
5.04	Temporary Suspension of Trading Under Registrant's Employee Benefit Plans
5.05	Amendments to the Registrant's Code of Ethics, or Waiver of a Provision of the Code of Ethics
5.06	Change in Shell Company Status
5.07	Submission of Matters to a Vote of Security Holders
5.08	Shareholder Director Nominations
7.01	Regulation FD Disclosure
8.01	Other Events
9.01	Financial Statements and Exhibits

(e) Proxy Statements:

Prepared in accordance with Regulation 14A for all proxy solicitations, detailing the matters to be voted on by shareholders, and including critical information about the company's executive compensation, board of directors, and auditors.

(f) Annual Report to Shareholders:

Often integrated with the Form 10-K, this document is a key communication tool for investors, providing a comprehensive overview of the company's performance, financials, and future outlook.

(g) Regulation FD:

This regulation ensures that all material information is disseminated to the public simultaneously to prevent selective disclosure to certain groups.

(h) Filing Deadlines:

Companies must adhere to strict deadlines for their SEC filings, which vary based on their filer status (accelerated, large accelerated, or non-accelerated filer).

(i) Signature and Certification Protocols:

The Form 10-K, in particular, requires not only signatures

from the company's principal officers and board members but also certification by the CEO and CFO, underscoring the importance of accuracy and accountability in financial reporting.

(j) **E-Proxy Rules:**

These rules modernize the proxy voting process by requiring the posting of proxy materials online and offering companies choices in how they deliver these materials to shareholders.

By meticulously preparing and submitting these documents, a company demonstrates its commitment to transparency, investor protection, and adherence to the rigorous standards set by the SEC, paving the way for a successful listing and ongoing investor relations.

5.2 Fiduciary Duties of Officers in Periodic Reporting: An In-Depth Look

The responsibilities of a company's officers, particularly the principal executive officer (PEO) and principal financial officer (PFO), are pivotal when it comes to the accuracy and integrity of periodic reports such as the Form 10-K and Form 10-Q. These officers are tasked with the following key obligations:

(a) Certifications Under Section 302:

The PEO and PFO must personally review each report filed.

They must attest that, to their knowledge, the report is truthful, does not contain any materially misleading statements, and includes all material facts necessary for a fair presentation of the company's financial status and performance during the period covered by the report.

(b) Financial Statement Integrity:

Officers must ensure that the financial statements and other financial information accurately reflect the company's financial condition, results of operations, and cash flows.

(c) Responsibility for Disclosure Controls and Procedures:

They must establish and maintain effective disclosure controls and procedures designed to make known to them any material information relating to the company and its subsidiaries.

o

(d) Internal Control Over Financial Reporting:

Officers are responsible for designing internal controls that provide reasonable assurance regarding the reliability of financial reporting and the preparation of financial statements in accordance with GAAP.

(e) **Evaluation of Disclosure Controls and Procedures:**

> At least 90 days before the report filing, they must evaluate the effectiveness of the company's disclosure controls and procedures and report their conclusions in the filing.

(f) **Disclosure of Changes and Deficiencies:**

> Any changes in the company's internal control over financial reporting that materially affect, or are reasonably likely to affect, the company's ability to report financial information must be disclosed.
>
> Officers must also report any significant deficiencies or material weaknesses in the design or operation of internal controls, as well as any fraud involving management or employees with a significant role in these controls.

(g) **Communication with Auditors and Audit Committee:**

> Officers must keep auditors and the audit committee informed about significant deficiencies and material weaknesses in internal controls, as well as any fraud that could impact the company's financial reporting.

(h) **Section 906 Certifications:**

> Officers must certify that the periodic report fully complies with the Securities Exchange Act's requirements

and that the information presented fairly represents the company's financial condition and results of operations.

These obligations underscore the critical role of the PEO and PFO in ensuring the transparency, accuracy, and reliability of a company's financial reporting. Their certifications serve as a linchpin of investor confidence and regulatory compliance.

5.3 Consequences of Non-Compliance: A Look at the Penalties for Violating SEC Certification Requirements

The legal framework surrounding the certification of financial reports by corporate officers is designed to enforce strict adherence to the truth and to maintain the integrity of financial disclosures. Here are the potential penalties for violations:

(a) Criminal Penalties Under Section 906:

Knowingly providing a false certification is a criminal offense, punishable by a fine of up to $1 million and imprisonment for up to 10 years.

Willfully providing a false certification, with the intent to defraud, is punishable by a fine of up to $5 million and imprisonment for up to 20 years.

(b) Civil and Criminal Penalties for Section 302 Violations:

Officers providing false Section 302 certifications can face penalties from the SEC for violating the anti-fraud provisions of the Securities Exchange Act, specifically Section 13(a) or 15(d).

They may also be subject to legal action from private litigants for violations of Section 10(b) of the Securities Exchange Act and Rule 10b-5, which prohibits fraudulent activities in connection with the purchase or sale of securities.

(c) **Increased Litigation Risk:**

Public certifications can increase the likelihood of officers being personally named as defendants in lawsuits brought by shareholders under Section 10(b) of the Securities Exchange Act.

Officers may also face derivative lawsuits, which are brought by shareholders on behalf of the corporation, alleging that the corporation suffered harm due to the officers' misconduct.

(d) **Forfeiture of Compensation Under Sarbanes-Oxley Section 304:**

If a company is required to restate its financial statements due to misconduct, officers must forfeit any bonuses, incentive-based or equity-based compensation, and profits from the sale of company securities received during the 12-month period following the initial issuance or filing of the restated financials.

These penalties serve as a strong deterrent against fraudulent financial reporting and underscore the seriousness with which regulatory authorities view the integrity of the financial certification process. Officers who sign these certifications assume a significant responsibility and must ensure the accuracy and completeness of the information they are attesting to.

5.4 Unstructured Disclosure Obligations: The Dynamics of Material Events and Communication

Beyond the structured disclosures mandated by the SEC through periodic reports, public companies also have unstructured disclosure obligations that arise from the need to maintain fair and efficient markets. These obligations are not explicitly outlined in the federal securities laws but are inferred from the general anti-fraud provisions, particularly Rule 10b-5 under the Securities Exchange Act.

Key Aspects of Unstructured Disclosure Obligations Include:

(a) Duty to Disclose:

Public companies must disclose material facts promptly, especially when insiders are trading in the company's securities. Insider trading is only permissible when material nonpublic information is already available to the public.

(b) Duty to Correct:

If a company has made an unstructured disclosure, it must ensure that the information remains accurate and complete. The company is obligated to update or correct any previous disclosures that are still relevant to investors but are no longer accurate due to changed circumstances or initial errors.

(c) Handling Rumors:

While there is no general duty to address rumors, a company may have a responsibility to respond or verify if it has some control or responsibility over the rumor or market report in question.

(d) Materiality:

The disclosure obligation is qualified by the concept of "materiality." Information is only required to be disclosed if it is material — that is, if a reasonable investor would consider it important to their investment decision.

(e) Examples of Material Events:

Events like significant mergers or acquisitions, stock splits, dividend policy changes, management changes, borrowing of significant funds, revenue or profit fluctuations, new contracts, product developments, and significant litigation or regulatory proceedings are typically considered material.

(f) Accuracy and Completeness:

All public disclosures, whether structured or unstructured, must be accurate and complete. This applies to public announcements, speeches, media interviews, press releases, analyst presentations, and even responses to telephone inquiries.

(g) Regulation FD Compliance:

Companies must coordinate their communications to ensure compliance with Regulation FD, which mandates that material information is disseminated to all investors simultaneously to prevent selective disclosure.

(h) Timing of Disclosure:

While immediate disclosure is generally required upon recognizing a duty to disclose, there are limited circumstances where delayed disclosure may be permitted, such as when serving a legitimate corporate purpose or when the information is unverified or unverifiable.

(i) Stock Exchange and FINRA Obligations:

For companies listed on a stock exchange, there are also contractual obligations to make timely public disclosures of material information, as mandated by the exchange or FINRA, which may exceed federal securities law requirements.

In summary, unstructured disclosure obligations are an integral part of a public company's responsibilities, ensuring that investors have access to material information in a timely and accurate manner. The management of public companies must carefully assess each situation to determine the disclosure duties and act accordingly to maintain the integrity of the capital markets.

5.5 Regulation FD and Analyst Communications: Ensuring Fair Disclosure

Regulation Fair Disclosure (FD) is a cornerstone of U.S. securities law that aims to ensure all investors have equal access to material information. Here's how it affects your ability to discuss company matters with analysts:

(a) Equal Access to Information:

Regulation FD mandates that when material, nonpublic information is intentionally disclosed to certain individuals, including securities professionals and investors likely to trade on this information, the company must also disclose this information to the general public simultaneously.

(b) Unintentional Disclosures:

If material, nonpublic information is unintentionally disclosed, the company must make it public promptly, which means as soon as reasonably practicable, but no later than 24 hours after the senior official learns of the disclosure or by the start of the next day's trading.

(c) Methods of Public Disclosure:

Public disclosure can be achieved by filing a Form 8-K with the SEC or through other methods designed to broadly distribute the information. This could include press releases, news wire services, press conferences, or public conference calls.

(d) Company Website as a Disclosure Tool:

Information posted on a company's website can satisfy Regulation FD obligations if it meets the SEC's three-part test:

- The website is a recognized channel of distribution.

- The posting disseminates information to the general securities marketplace.

- A reasonable waiting period is provided for market reaction.

(e) Limitations on Private Discussions:

While Regulation FD does not prohibit one-on-one meetings with analysts, it does require that any material information shared during these meetings be disclosed to the public as described above. This prevents selective disclosure and ensures all investors have access to the same information.

(f) Ongoing Monitoring and Compliance:

Companies must monitor their communications with analysts and investors to ensure ongoing compliance with Regulation FD. This includes training executives and employees on the regulation's requirements and implementing communication protocols.

(g) Consequences of Non-Compliance:

Failure to comply with Regulation FD can result in SEC enforcement actions, reputational harm, and potential legal liabilities.

By understanding and adhering to Regulation FD, companies can maintain fair and transparent communication practices with analysts and all investors, fostering trust and confidence in the marketplace.

5.6 Dancing with Regulation FD: A Playful Guide to

Capitalizing on Dreams: Guide to U.S. IPO & Listings Compliance

Embrace the rhythm of Regulation Fair Disclosure (FD) with a zest that ensures all investors waltz to the same tune of information. Here's how to make sure you and your company swing to the beat of this regulatory standard:

(a) Craft a Whimsical Written Policy:

Whip up a written disclosure policy that's as colorful as a storybook, detailing the company's chatty practices with all the enchanting clarity.

(b) Choose Your Speakers Wisely:

Handpick a select group of speakers who get to chat with those covered by Regulation FD. Let everyone else know they're part of the silent chorus unless they get the nod to sing.

(c) Master the Earnings Release Ritual:

Choreograph a consistent dance for quarterly earnings releases and interim earnings warnings. Consider a detailed press release that swings open its doors to any upcoming analyst call. Broadcast the call or webcast to all, kick it off with safe harbor language, and script the presentation and Q&As like a Broadway show. Afterwards, remember to keep all the scripts and track records on file for the record and for others to look back and / or review.

(d) Be a Factual Fixer, Not a Critic:

Limit your review of draft analysts' reports to being a grammar guru and a fact-checker. Keep your comments to factual errors and refrain from critiquing the analysis or model. Don't distribute or sponsor any analysts' reports as if they were your own.

(e) Script the Investor Conference Performance:

Make presentations at investor conferences as scripted as a stage play. Keep the presenter on track and avoid breakout sessions that could lead to off-script adlibs. Consider webcasting the presentation to a wider, virtual audience.

(f) Beware the Bottom Line Boondoggle:

Be cautious with providing earnings guidance. Keep any guidance in communications crisp and clear via press releases and conference calls. Avoid using old "we are comfortable" phrases unless they refer to past company guidance. Steer clear of "walking the street" with guidance on a selective basis.

o

(g) Update at Your Own Discretion:

Make it clear that any forward-looking statements are not

on a constant update loop due to new developments or otherwise.

(h) Ink Non-Disclosure Agreements:

Use written non-disclosure agreements for those privy to inside information. These agreements should also put a lock on trading in the company's securities until the info goes public.

(i) Follow the Non-GAAP Measures Tune:

Make sure to comply with the rules for the disclosure of non-GAAP financial measures, keeping your financial reporting in harmony with regulatory melodies.

(j) Display Your Policies for All to See:

Post the company's Regulation FD disclosure policies on its website like a proud marquee, ensuring everyone knows the steps to this regulatory dance.

By following these playful yet precise steps, your company can ensure that it not only complies with Regulation FD but does so with a flourish that keeps the investor relations dance floor lively and fair for all.

5.7 The High Stakes of Skipping the Regulation FD Waltz: A Look at the Consequences

Neglecting the playful yet precise steps of Regulation Fair Disclosure (FD) isn't just a misstep in the dance of investor relations—it's a potential pitfall that can lead to serious consequences. Here's what can happen if a company fails to twirl to the tune of Regulation FD:

(a) No Solo Performances:

Not making the required public disclosures doesn't automatically break Rule 10b-5's rulebook. Regulation FD doesn't grant individuals the power to sue; it's a dance only the SEC can lead to the courtroom.

(b) Confusion is Not an Option:

The SEC has its eyes peeled for disclosures that are as confusing as a mislabeled ballroom. If a company's disclosures are misleading or a puzzle to investors, the SEC may step in with an enforcement action.

(c) Crafting Clarity:

It's crucial for companies to pen their disclosures with the finesse of a poet and the precision of a lawyer, ensuring the public is not only informed but also enlightened.

(d) Enforcement Actions:

The SEC has been the maestro of numerous enforcement actions for Regulation FD violations, playing the tune of compliance for public companies and their executives.

(e) Cease-and-Desist Orders:

The SEC can impose cease-and-desist orders, effectively pressing the pause button on non-compliant behavior and demanding a return to the path of regulatory harmony.

(f) Fining the Fumble:

Significant civil fines can be levied, making the cost of non-compliance more than just a loss of reputation—it hits the pocketbook, too.

(g) Regulation FD in the Spotlight:

Regulation FD remains a star in the SEC's enforcement show, with the regulator keen on ensuring that all companies perform their part in the ballet of fair disclosure.

In this high-stakes dance, where information is the rhythm and compliance is the step, companies must move with grace and precision to avoid the missteps that can lead to the SEC's stern gaze. By keeping in time with Regulation FD, companies can ensure they keep the investor relations dance floor both fair and lively.

5.8 Guarding the Garden: Preventive Measures Against Insider Trading

Capitalizing on Dreams: Guide to U.S. IPO & Listings

Insider trading is a thicket that companies and their insiders must navigate with care, lest they find themselves ensnared in a tangle of legal and ethical thorns. Here's how to cultivate a garden of compliance and keep the insider trading beast at bay:

(a) Educate, Don't Intimidate:

Illuminate the minds of directors, officers, and employees with knowledge of the "insider trading" laws. Let them see the light of ethical conduct and shield themselves and the company from the quagmire of civil or criminal liability.

(b) Adopt a Policy as Strong as a Hedge:

Craft insider trading policies that are as firm as an oak, prohibiting trading on material, nonpublic information or "tipping" others to trade. This policy should be the first line of defense against the siren song of insider trading.

(c) Blackout Periods and Window Periods:

Introduce "blackout periods" when insiders are barred from trading in company securities, or "window periods" when trading is permissible, but only if not armed with material, nonpublic information.

(d) Internal Procedures as a Shield:

Adopt policies and programs tailored to the company's unique tapestry, designed to prevent insider trading. These procedures can serve as a shield against liability under the "reckless disregard" standard.

(e) Compliance Program Components:

Weave a tapestry of compliance that includes:

- Education for officers and employees.

- Obligations of confidentiality.

- Procedures for engaging with the media and investment community, in harmony with the company's Regulation FD disclosure policy.

- Trading windows and pre-clearance procedures for certain individuals.

(f) Rule 10b5-1 Trading Plans:

Consider the art of Rule 10b5-1 trading plans, allowing executives to schedule future stock sales without the constraints of insider trading policies. These plans, when crafted while free of inside information, provide a legal safe harbor even amidst a sea of material, nonpublic information.

(g) Crafting the Rule 10b5-1 Plan:

To be effective, the plan must be written and meet three criteria:

- First, specify the number of shares to be bought or sold.

- Second, indicate the price at which shares will be transacted, whether by a fixed price, limit order, or market price.

- Third, include the timing of the trades, whether by a set date, time, or contingent event.

(h) Transparency in Trading Plans:

If a company adopts such plans, consider shining a light on their existence and noting in the executives' Form 4 filings when sales are made according to the Rule 10b5-1 plans.

By following these steps, a company can create a fortress of compliance, protecting its reputation and ensuring that the delicate dance of the capital markets is performed with integrity and fairness for all participants.

5.9 The Heavy Hand of Justice: Penalties for Securities Fraud Unveiled

Capitalizing on Dreams: Guide to U.S. IPO & Listings

Veering off the straight and narrow onto the winding roads of securities fraud? The Sarbanes-Oxley Act has its eyes on you, with a stern gaze and an even sterner set of penalties. Here's what the law has to say about those who'd dare to defraud:

(a) New Criminal Anti-Fraud Provisions:

The Act weaves a new criminal net, capturing anyone who schemes or artfully deceives in the realm of securities registered under the Securities Exchange Act. It's not just about defrauding others but also about illicitly obtaining money or property through false pretenses.

(b) Broadened Prosecution and Enhanced Penalties:

This legal tapestry broadens the weave of criminal prosecution for securities fraud, casting a wider net and increasing the severity of penalties for those caught in its threads.

(c) Increased Criminal Penalties:

The Act ups the ante for mail fraud, wire fraud, and other anti-fraud violations of the Securities Exchange Act, making sure the price of dishonesty is steep.

(d) Civil Liability for Insiders:

Insiders who find themselves on the wrong side of the anti-fraud provisions can also face civil liability, with the

Sarbanes-Oxley Act extending the statute of limitations for private claims of fraud, deceit, or manipulation.

(e) Extended Statute of Limitations:

The timeline for asserting a private claim has been stretched to the earlier of two years after discovery or five years after the violation, a significant lengthening from the previous one and three-year window.

(f) SEC's Escrow Order Power:

In the midst of an investigation, the SEC can slap a temporary order on a company to escrow any extraordinary payments to employees or agents for 45 days, with the possibility of a court-ordered extension if good cause is shown.

(g) Non-Dischargeable Debts in Bankruptcy:

A particularly heavy blow: individual debts resulting from securities law violations or common law fraud are no longer erased in bankruptcy, clinging like a shadow that won't dissipate.

The Sarbanes-Oxley Act serves as a bulwark against securities fraud, fortifying the justice system's ability to penalize and prosecute those who would game the system. For those who might consider such a path, the road ahead is fraught with legal perils and the promise of severe repercussions.

5.10 The Playbook of Integrity: Navigating the Foreign Corrupt Practices Act

The Foreign Corrupt Practices Act (FCPA) isn't just a rulebook; it's a beacon guiding U.S. companies through the murky waters of international business with a spotlight of integrity. Here's the playbook for staying on the straight and narrow:

(a) No Bribery Allowed:

The FCPA slams the door on bribery of foreign government officials, a firm no-no for all U.S. companies seeking to play fair in the global market.

(b) Accounting Provisions:

It's not just about actions but records too. Issuers must keep books, records, and accounts that are like a detailed diary, accurately reflecting all transactions and asset dispositions, regardless of where they occur.

(c) Recording with a Purpose:

Records should be more than just numbers; they should tell a story that could flag any potential illegality or impropriety. Mislabeling bribes as "sales commissions"? That's a big red flag that the FCPA is watching for.

(d) Internal Accounting Controls:

Issuers are tasked with devising and maintaining a system that serves up reasonable assurances that transactions are authorized and recorded properly, like a well-guarded fortress with only the king's permission to move the treasure.

(e) Prudent Officials' Standard:

The records and controls should be so robust that they would satisfy even the most prudent of officials managing their own affairs, as if their personal wealth was at stake.

(f) SEC Rules Under FCPA:

The SEC has added its own layers to the FCPA, prohibiting any falsification of books or records and preventing directors or officers from making false or misleading statements to accountants, especially during audits or SEC filings.

By adhering to the FCPA's requirements, companies can ensure they compete globally not just with the strength of their products or services, but with the strength of their character, building trust and reputation that money can't buy. After all, in the game of business, integrity isn't just a rule— it's a winning strategy.

Capitalizing on Dreams: Guide to U.S. IPO & Listings

5.11 Tiptoeing Through the Tulips: A Whimsical Look at Insider Trading Regulations

In the whimsical world of securities laws, Rule 10b-5 under the Securities Exchange Act is the gardener, tending to the rich soil of fair trade. It blooms with a ban on any person using cunning devices, schemes, or artifice to defraud, like a mischievous fox in a tale, or telling fibs about material facts, or even leaving out crucial details that would change the whole story.

This rule has been seen as a fence around the company's garden, preventing officers, directors, and affiliates from plucking the fruits of "inside" information—those juicy nonpublic facts—until they've been shared with everyone under the sun and time has passed for the news to spread like wildfire.

Imagine selling or buying securities right after announcing a big, important fact (without a carefully crafted Rule 10b5-1 plan in place). That could be seen as a dance with the devil under Rule 10b-5. Some say three business days after a public announcement is like a golden rule, but sometimes, hot news travels faster, and complex deals might need more time to simmer down.

Now, picture the Insider Trading Sanctions Act of 1984, a vigilant guardian, making sure that anyone who trades on secret info, or tips others to do so, faces a civil penalty. This penalty? Up to three times the profit made or loss dodged from such a naughty trade. The SEC can come knocking with this penalty and more, including criminal charges.

This act extends its long arm to all transactions, except public offerings, through the national securities exchange or via brokers or dealers. It even includes derivative securities like options, warrants, and the likes. And oh, those who pass on the secret info (tippers) are just as liable as the traders (tippnees).

Then there's the Insider Trading and Securities Fraud Enforcement Act of 1988, a stern sibling to the Insider Act, imposing penalties on controlling persons. Even if they don't personally gain from the insider activity, they could face a penalty of $1 million or three times the profit or loss avoided. This act takes a broad view of "controlling persons," including anyone with power to influence, even if not exerted.

Remember, being in compliance with the Securities Act or Rule 10b-5 doesn't shield you from insider trading liability, and it certainly doesn't stop Section 16(b) from being applicable. So, tread lightly, dear traders, and keep your garden of trades fair and square for all.

5.12 The Symphony of Section 16: A Playful Guide to SEC Filings

In the grand theater of the Securities Exchange Act, Section 16(a) takes the stage as our maestro, conducting a symphony of obligations for the officers, directors, and select shareholders of public companies. Let's turn the pages of this playful guide and see what melodies these insiders must play:

(a) The Baton Twirl: Reporting Transactions

Section 16(a) and (b) are the twin batons of this act. While (a) swirls around the reporting of transactions in company securities, (b) dances to the tune of disgorging short-swing profits—those gained from a quickstep sale and purchase within a six-month jig.

(b) Casting the Insiders

The spotlight shines on every director, executive officer, and any person who holds more than 10% of the company's equity securities, all bound to play by Section 16's rules.

(c) Defining the Maestro's Circle

The SEC's rulebook defines "officer" to include the president, principal financial officer, and other key players in the company's policy-making orchestra.

(d) Beneficial Ownership: The Key to the Kingdom

The concept of beneficial ownership is the golden ticket to Section 16's requirements, focusing on who has the power to vote or invest in the company's securities.

(e) The Two-Act Beneficial Ownership Play

The first act uses beneficial ownership to identify the greater than 10% shareholders. The second act, based on "pecuniary interest," determines which transactions must be reported and are up for potential profit sharing.

(f) The Grand Entrance: Initial Statement of Beneficial Ownership

With Form 3, insiders make their grand entrance, filing an "Initial Statement of Beneficial Ownership" within 10 days of assuming their role.

(g) The Quickstep: Form 4 Filings

When an insider acquires or disposes of any equity securities, they must quickstep to Form 4, filing it within two business days of the transaction.

(h) The Curtain Call: Reporting Changes

If an officer or director exits the stage, they must still file a Form 4 to report any changes in beneficial ownership that occurred within six months of their departure.

(i) The Audience Watches: SEC Monitoring and Public Perception

The SEC and the public are the audience, watching the

insiders' every move through Form 4 filings, which help monitor for foul play and offer insights into the company's prospects.

(j) The Encore: Proxy Statement Disclosures

The company must give an encore in its proxy statement, disclosing the names of any insiders who failed to file or were late to the game.

By following this playful guide, insiders can ensure they perform in harmony with the SEC's expectations, avoiding the discord of penalties or the silent treatment from the investing public. So, let the music play, and let the filings be timely and accurate!

5.13 The Whirlwind of Section 16(b): A Lighthearted Look at Short-Swing Profits

In the spirited world of the Securities Exchange Act, Section 16(b) leaps onto the stage with a spirited twirl, casting a watchful eye on officers, directors, and shareholders who hold more than 10% of the company's stock. Let's dance through the lighthearted look at the disgorgement provisions that Section 16(b) brings to the table:

(a) The Quickstep of Profits:

Section 16(b) is all about the quickstep dance of buying and selling (or selling and buying) company stock within a flirtatious six-month period, capturing any "short-swing profits" that may arise from these nimble-footed moves.

(b) The Six-Month Waltz:

This six-month measure can be counted from the date of any transaction, pirouetting backward or forward, making no assumptions about which foot falls first—purchase or sale.

(c) The Proposed May Transactions:

Imagine a sale in May followed by a purchase in July, or vice versa. Both would find themselves twirling under Section 16(b)'s watchful gaze, even if the transactions occurred before or after one's tenure as an officer or director.

(d) Exemptions from the Dance:

Grants of options, stock awards, and certain other acquisitions are generally exempt from this dance, as long as they satisfy the traditional six-month holding period.

(e) The Option Exercise Two-Step:

The SEC rules consider the grant of a stock option (not its exercise) a "purchase," allowing officers and directors to exercise options and sell the stock immediately without worrying about disgorging profits, provided they've held the options for at least six months.

(f) Liability for the Unintentional Tango:

Insiders may find themselves liable for short-swing profits, whether or not they intended to dance this tango. If a court spots a "profit" from any two transactions within the six-month window, that profit, along with any legal fees from the collection rumba, must be handed over to the company.

(g) The Profit Calculation Conga Line:

Determining the existence and amount of profit is a complex dance with many steps, and the method that results in the maximum liability will be the one that's chosen to lead the conga line.

(h) The Unplanned Pas de Trois:

Often, insiders find themselves caught in the Section 16(b) net not out of a desire for quick profit, but due to inadvertence, oversight, or a lack of proper planning by the company or the shareholder.

So, let the music play and the dance continue, but remember, in the world of Section 16(b), every step must be carefully considered to avoid an unintended whirlwind of profits returning to the company's coffers.

5.14 Tiptoeing Through the Tulips: Insider Trading and Short Sales

In the charming meadow of the Securities Exchange Act, Section 16(c) gently places a fence around the flowerbed of short sales, making it unlawful for insiders to dance this particular jig. Let's take a whimsical walk through this particular patch of regulations:

(a) A Firm No-Go:

Section 16(c) lays down the law, stating that insiders can only sell the blossoms of stock they own, not borrowed blooms. And even then, they must deliver them promptly, like a well-timed handshake.

(b) The Garden of Ownership:

Insiders are invited to trade in the garden of stocks they possess. Borrowing and selling other's flowers—what some might call "short selling" or "sale against the box"—is strictly off-limits.

(c) The Seed of Presumption:

The heart of this rule blooms from a presumption that insiders might pluck short sales from the vine of inside information, information that, if it were to see the light of day, would wilt the market price of the company's securities.

(d) A Thorny Tangle:

Engaging in a short sale not only breaks Section 16(c) but could also tangle the insider in potential Section 16(b) problems and a bramble patch of anti-fraud rule inquiries.

So, while the markets are a garden of opportunities, insiders must tend their trades with care, avoiding the thorny paths of short sales and staying within the sunny lanes of fair dealing. After all, in the garden of business, only the fairest flowers should be plucked and traded.

5.15 The Grand Reveal: Unveiling Significant Shareholders' Reporting Chore

Beyond the enchanting realm of Section 16, the Securities Exchange Act beckons significant shareholders to take center stage with a flourish of reporting requirements, as dictated by Sections 13(d) and 13(g). Let's twirl through the details with a touch of whimsy:

(a) The 5% Milestone:

Imagine a garden where only those tending more than 5% of the company's stock are invited to perform. For these special gardeners, a grand entrance is required, filing a Schedule 13D or 13G with the SEC upon first crossing the 5% threshold.

(b) The Dance of Disclosure:

Once a significant shareholder, always a dancer in the ballet of disclosure. Any material changes in ownership must be followed by amended filings, waltzing through the SEC's corridors with the latest updates.

(c) The Group Gala:

When two or more individuals join hands to form a group for the purpose of acquiring, holding, or disposing of 5% or more of the company's stock, they collectively become the star of the show, a "person" under the Act's gaze.

(d) The Agreement Waltz:

The moment two or more agree to synchronize their steps, they form a group. On the date of this agreement, the group is deemed to have beneficially owned all the company's stock held by its members.

(e) The Collective Choreography:

The group must move as one, filing collectively and ensuring that their collective ownership is known and updated, reflecting the collective power of their shared garden plot.

In this grand performance, significant shareholders and their groups are not merely spectators but active participants, ensuring transparency and fair play in the garden of the capital markets. With each filing, they contribute to the symphony of information that keeps the market's rhythm in sync and its melody in tune.

5.16 Unlocking the Vault: Insider Share Sales Post-IPO

After the curtain call of an Initial Public Offering (IPO), the question on every insider's mind is, can they start their own encore by selling their shares? Let's spin a tale of regulations and unlock the mysteries surrounding insider share sales.

(a) The Restricted Seating:

The resale of restricted securities is akin to a VIP area with limited access. Insiders can't just waltz in and sell their shares unless (1) there's an effective registration statement for those shares, or (2) they've got a legal green light that registration is unnecessary.

(b) The Origins of Restriction:

A stock becomes "restricted" in two main ways: either it's a private placement direct from the company or an affiliate, or it's sold privately by an affiliate.

(c) The Company's Treasury:

The company itself can't sell or offer to sell any securities, including those in its treasury, without registering the transaction under the Securities Act. This rule applies to both equity, like stocks, and debt securities.

(d) Exemptions from Registration:

But the company isn't always required to register a transaction if the Securities Act provides a specific exemption, often for "private placements" that don't involve a public offering.

(e) The Private Placement Prelude:

A "private placement" is like a secret concert for a select few, where securities are sold to a limited number of qualified investors who pledge to keep their tickets (securities) for the long haul.

(f) Control Securities and Affiliates:

All securities owned by "affiliates" of the company are called "control securities" and are subject to similar limitations. They can generally only be sold in a registered offering, unless an exemption applies.

(g) Common Exemptions:

The most common exemptions from registration for control securities are (1) a sale under Rule 144, and (2) a non-statutory private sale, similar to the company's private placement.

(h) The FAST Act's Fresh Breeze:

In December 2015, the FAST Act added a new registration exemption for private resales of securities, like a sudden gust of wind that changes the direction of a sail.

(i) Defining "Affiliates":

An "affiliate" is anyone who has the power to control or is controlled by the issuer, or shares common control. This includes directors, officers, and major shareholders, along with their familial and business connections.

So, while the IPO is a grand stage for the company, the insiders must tread carefully when it comes to selling their shares. With the right permissions and exemptions, they can eventually join the market's dance, but until then, they watch from the wings.

5.17 Unlocking the Insider's Share Sale Safari: A Rule 144 Expedition

Dive into the delightful world of stock trading with a touch of legal finesse, where Rule 144 opens up a treasure trove of opportunities for insiders to sell their shares without the cumbersome process of registering them under the Securities Act. It's like having a secret passage in a maze, allowing you to navigate with ease and elegance.

Capitalizing on Dreams: Guide to U.S. IPO & Listings

Think of Rule 144 as your trusty sidekick, providing a "safe harbor" from the registration requirements, not the only one in town, but certainly a popular choice. It's the go-to rule when you're ready to sell your control securities or restricted securities, as long as you play by its rules.

Let's break down the fun steps:

(a) Volume Limit:

It's all about moderation. Rule 144 sets a cap on how much you can sell in a three-month period. It's a friendly competition between (1) one percent of the outstanding shares of the same class you're selling, or (2) the average weekly trading volume in the same class during the four weeks before you file the notice of sale. It's like choosing between your favorite dessert or the most popular one in town.

(b) Form 144:

If you're planning to sell more than 5,000 shares or if the sales price is over $50,000, you'll need to file a notice of sale on Form 144 with the SEC and the relevant national securities exchange. It's like sending out an invitation to a grand sale, but with all the formalities in place.

(c) Only Certain Transactions Qualify:

Your sale must be as ordinary as a cup of morning coffee, meaning it's a straightforward brokerage transaction. The broker is there to serve you, taking only the usual commission and not playing any extra games. They'll also do a "reasonable inquiry" to ensure everything is on the up and up, documented with a questionnaire and a letter from you, the seller, confirming compliance with Rule 144.

(d) Holding Period:

If you're selling restricted securities, you must have owned them beneficially for at least six months, provided the issuer has been reporting to the Securities Exchange Act for 90 days before the sale. If not, it's a one-year holding period. It's like waiting for a fine wine to mature before you can enjoy its full flavor.

(e) Using Securities as Collateral:

Can you use your securities as collateral for a bank loan? Absolutely, as long as it's done in good faith. If there's a default, the bank's sale can be counted with your own for a year when calculating volume limits. It's like having a safety net that also counts towards your sales record.

(f) Gifts and Donations:

What about giving stocks as gifts? Sales by the recipients can also be aggregated with your sales for up to a year after the gift. It's the spirit of giving with a touch of legal compliance.

(g) Section 4(a)(2) and the "Section 4(a)(1 ½)" exemption:

This is where things get really interesting. It's an exemption for transactions by an issuer that doesn't involve a public offering. The SEC has taken a "no action" stance for private sales by controlling persons that meet some of the requirements of this exemption and Rule 144. It's like having a secret handshake that lets you pass through certain doors.

(h) FAST Act and Section 4(a)(7):

The FAST Act added a new layer to the game with Section 4(a)(7), offering a safe harbor for private resales under the "Section 4(a)(1 ½)" exemption. It's like discovering a new shortcut in your favorite video game.

So there you have it—a delightful journey through the world of insider stock sales with Rule 144, where compliance and creativity go hand in hand, ensuring that your path to selling shares is as smooth and enjoyable as a well-crafted story.

5.18 Can Employees Cash in on Pre-IPO Shares? A Quick Jaunt Through Rule 701 and Rule 144

Imagine you're a gardener who's been given a handful of seeds (shares) as part of your compensation. You've nurtured

Capitalizing on Dreams: Guide to U.S. IPO & Listings

these seeds, and now they're about to blossom into a beautiful garden (IPO). But can you sell these flowers before the grand opening? Let's take a fun-filled romp through the rules to find out!

(a) Rule 701: The Greenhouse for Shares

Rule 701 is like a greenhouse, providing a warm and regulated environment for private companies to grow their seeds (offer and sell securities) to their gardeners (employees) as part of their compensation. This exemption from registration allows companies to issue shares to their employees in the years leading up to the big bloom (IPO).

(b) Restricted Securities: The Need for Care

The seeds you receive are special; they're considered 'restricted securities.' This means they come with certain rules about when and how they can be sold. You can't just rush to the market and sell them; you need to follow a proper path, like using a registration statement filed by the company or finding a valid exemption.

(c) Enter Rule 144: The Path to Selling

When your company starts to show its flowers to the world (becomes subject to the Securities Exchange Act reporting requirements), and has done so for at least 90 days, you, as an employee, can start thinking about selling your shares. Rule 144 comes to the rescue, allowing you to resell your shares without being bound by the usual holding period restrictions.

(d) The 90-Day Milestone: From Greenhouse to Garden

Once your company has been reporting to the Securities Exchange Act for 90 days, it's like the greenhouse has been opened to the outdoors. The restrictions on your shares start to loosen, and you can consider selling them under Rule 144. This is the moment you've been waiting for, where your seeds can be transformed into a bouquet of benefits.

So, to answer the question, yes, employees can sell shares issued under an employee benefit plan prior to an IPO, but they must wait until the company has been reporting under the Securities Exchange Act for 90 days and then follow the exemption pathways like Rule 144 to do so legally and smoothly.

It's like a well-planned garden party where everything has its time and place, and when done right, it can be a delightful celebration of growth and prosperity for both the company and its employees.

5.19 SOX Safari: Crafting a Public Company's Document Trail

Once upon a time, in the not-so-distant past of 2001 and 2002, the corporate world was shaken by scandals that cast a shadow over the business landscape. The cries of "Foul!" rang out as allegations surfaced that key documents were mysteriously vanishing, and investigations were hitting dead ends. It was a dark chapter in the annals of corporate governance, but fear not, for a hero emerged from the pages of legislation—the SOX!

This gallant Act swooped in like a knight in shining armor, not only reinforcing the existing rules but also layering on additional protections. It wove a rich tapestry, a mosaic of mandates, that dictate how public companies must treat their documents. It's not just about keeping papers safe; it's about the whole enchilada of document retention and destruction, and the proper conduct of companies and their employees under the watchful eyes of investigation.

The Pillars of SOX: A Wonderland of Compliance

(a) Section 302: The Heart of Truth

> This section is like the golden key that unlocks the castle of financial integrity. It requires the grand poobahs of the company, the CEOs and CFOs, to personally vouch for the accuracy of financial statements and the sturdiness of internal controls. It's like making them promise on their family's treasure chest that everything is on the up and up.

(b) Section 404: The Fortress of Internal Controls

Picture a moat filled with alligators and walls as high as the sky. That's what Section 404 is like. It demands that companies fortify their internal controls and reporting methods, ensuring that financial reports are as secure as a dragon's hoard.

(c) Section 802: The Time Capsule of Records

This section is like a wizard's spell that can preserve documents for a span of seven long years. It casts a net over all types of business records, ensuring they are kept safe from the destructive whims of those who might wish to alter history.

5.20 The Grand Adventure of Document Retention

In this grand adventure, public companies are the brave explorers, navigating through the dense jungle of compliance. They must create a document retention policy that is as delightful as it is interesting, ensuring that all documents are treated with the respect they deserve.

This policy is not just a dry list of rules; it's a vibrant map that guides the company through the treacherous terrain of legal and regulatory requirements. It's a tale of organization, security, and the wise management of information, where every document has a story to tell and a role to play in the company's history.

So, dear public company, as you embark on this quest,

remember that your document retention policy is your trusty steed. Ride it well, and let the Sarbanes-Oxley Act be your guide to a land where transparency and integrity reign supreme!

5.21 Preserve and Protect: The Document Duty Dance

In the intriguing world of corporate governance, there's a sly fox called "Duty to Preserve Documents" that companies must outwit. This crafty creature operates in three cunning stages, which we shall explore with the finesse of a seasoned dancer:

(a) The Waltz with Litigation or Investigation:

When the music of a lawsuit or probe has officially begun, it's time to do the document waltz. Companies must swirl their relevant documents onto the preservation dance floor, keeping them in their original form. It's a duty as strict as a tango, leaving no room for the two-left-feet shuffle.

(b) The Foxtrot of Foreseeable Legal Skirmishes:

Before the first note of a lawsuit or probe is played, if a company can sense the rhythm of potential legal action (reasonably foreseeable, that is), the duty to preserve documents may already be knocking at the door. This is especially true in complex transactions where regulatory approval dances to the beat of potential scrutiny. So, when the signs are clear, it's time to foxtrot those documents onto the preservation floor.

(c) **The Freestyle Fling in the Absence of Foreseeable Legal Tangos**:

When there's no litigation or investigation on the horizon, and no regulatory siren song calling for document retention, a company has the liberty to cha-cha its way through document disposal. But beware, for if a legal tango unexpectedly begins, any previous document destruction could be under the spotlight, with negative inferences dancing around like uninvited guests at a party.

Always remember, in the rearview mirror of corporate memory, litigation and investigations often appear on the horizon much sooner than they did in reality. So, tread carefully in the document duty dance, and you'll keep your company's steps light and your compliance in check. Preserve with prudence, and you'll avoid the tangle of legal trip-ups.

5.22 The High Stakes Game of Document Destruction: A Cautionary Tale

In the grand library of corporate responsibility, there's a sacred rule: don't play with fire by destroying documents that should be preserved. This rule is etched in stone for a reason, and those who break it might find themselves in a labyrinth of legal troubles.

(a) When the Civil Hammer Falls

If a company finds itself in the unenviable position of having destroyed documents it shouldn't have, the repercussions can be as varied as the circumstances surrounding the act. The severity of civil sanctions depends on the narrative of the misdeed. If the destruction was a deliberate attempt to erase evidence—what we might call 'bad faith'—then the legal eagles are more likely to swoop down with sanctions. But even a dance of negligence can lead to some form of penalty. The more the destruction harms the other party in a legal scuffle, the more likely it is that the sanctions will come knocking.

(b) The Criminal Gauntlet

Step beyond the bounds of civil into the shadowy realm of criminality, and the stakes rise dramatically. Federal statutes stand as sentinels, guarding against the obstruction of justice and the smooth operation of government proceedings. Woe to the company or individual who attempts to thwart these proceedings through the alteration or destruction of documents.

The Sarbanes-Oxley Act wields a particularly sharp sword against such transgressions. It turns the act of tampering with records into a criminal offense, one that can lead to a gauntlet of up to 20 years in prison. Whether it's altering, destroying, mutilating, concealing, falsifying, or any other form of creative record manipulation, the intent to impede an investigation or the administration of justice is a red line that should never be crossed.

In this high stakes game, ignorance is not bliss, and hindsight is 20/20. The prudent path is to tread carefully, to preserve documents as if they were precious artifacts, and to let transparency and compliance be the guiding stars. After all, in the intricate dance of corporate governance, it's better to have a document and not need it, than to need a document and not have it. So, keep those records safe, and may you always sleep soundly, knowing you've played by the rules.

5.23 Crafting a Risk-Ready Business

In the ebb and flow of business, **risk management** is the compass that guides companies through the unpredictable seas of commerce. For those on the cusp of an IPO, establishing robust systems for risk oversight is paramount. These systems must be as broad as they are deep, addressing both the economic headwinds and the unique challenges specific to the company's domain.

(a) Audit Committee as Risk Stewards

The audit committee often takes the lead in risk oversight, sometimes with a specialized subcommittee. Their role is to become the risk experts, educating the board on the full spectrum of potential impacts.

(b) Industry Experience in Risk Oversight

It's prudent to include a member with industry experience—someone who can navigate the known and hidden shoals of company-specific risks.

(c) Proactive Risk Management Systems

The committee ensures the company has systems that not only monitor but also anticipate and inform business decisions with current and future risk data.

(d) Communication: The Risk Management Lifeline

Effective risk oversight relies on the free flow of information, allowing insights to move from the deck to the bridge without hindrance.

(e) Regular Risk Assessment Meetings

Frequent meetings between the committee and risk management personnel are essential for strategic navigation and adaptation.

(f) Resilience Through Risk Management

Equipped with a solid risk management program, a company becomes a flagship of adaptability, ready to weather any storm. By staying vigilant and responsive, you set a course for sustainable success. Set your sails with the winds of risk management for a prosperous journey ahead!

5.24 SOX in a Nutshell: The Sarbanes-Oxley Act Explained

The Sarbanes-Oxley Act, a legislative lightning rod enacted in 2002, was designed to restore investor confidence following a string of corporate scandals. Here's the essence of SOX:

(a) Immediate Impact and SEC Role:

Some parts of SOX took effect immediately, while others needed the SEC to set the stage with additional rules.

(b) Accounting Overhaul:

SOX put the accounting profession under a new regulatory microscope, ensuring audits of public companies are more transparent and reliable.

(c) Legal Profession's Periphery:

Though not the main focus, SOX indirectly influenced the legal profession's role in corporate governance.

(d) Direct Corporate Effects:

For companies issuing securities, SOX mandated key reforms in financial reporting and corporate governance.

SOX is the financial world's integrity enforcer, ensuring transparency and accountability in the corporate sphere.

5.25 The Sarbanes-Oxley Act and Loans to Company Stewards

The SOX draws a clear line in the sand when it comes to loans to those at the helm of corporations—directors and executive officers. Let's break down the boundaries set by this legislative act:

(a) The Clear 'No Loan' Zone SOX

throws a regulatory net over companies, prohibiting them from offering, maintaining, arranging, or renewing loans to their directors, executive officers, and their affiliates. This rule is a universal one, applying to all public companies, whether they're listed on stock exchanges or not.

(b) Grandfathered Loans and the Line in the Sand

Any loans that were already in progress when SOX became law are allowed to continue, but they can't be significantly altered or renewed under the new rules. It's like a 'frozen in time' scenario for those pre-existing agreements.

(c) The Broad Stroke of 'Credit'

The term "credit" under SOX could be interpreted broadly, potentially encompassing financial arrangements beyond traditional loans. This might include third-party loans facilitated by the company, which could fall under the prohibition umbrella.

(d) A Firm 'No Guarantee' Rule

Companies are explicitly forbidden from backing the repayment of loans to their directors or executive officers. It's a clear-cut rule that ensures no hidden financial safety nets are in place for the corporate leaders.

(e) A Carve-out for Loan Companies

There's a notable exception for companies whose core business is lending. They're allowed to extend loans to directors and executive officers, but with a catch—private companies must repay any such loans before they can file a registration statement with the SEC.

(f) Private Companies and the Loan Landscape

While private companies aren't outright prohibited from making loans to their directors and officers, any new loans or significant modifications to existing ones after SOX became law must be repaid in full before the company can take steps towards going public.

In essence, SOX has tightened the financial reins on public

companies, ensuring that the relationship between corporate leaders and the entities they serve remains transparent and free from potential conflicts of interest. It's a legislative act that promotes financial integrity and corporate responsibility.

5.26 SOX's Audit Committee Standards: A Concise Guide

The SOX issued a clarion call for transparency and integrity, especially in how audit committees operate. Here's a snapshot of the standards it imposes:

(a) Independence Mandate

SOX requires audit committees of listed companies to be composed entirely of independent directors, with only a few narrow exceptions. To qualify as independent, members must pass a two-pronged test:

- **No Extra Fees:** Audit committee members cannot receive consulting, advisory, or compensatory fees from the company, other than their director's pay. This rule extends to indirect payments as well, including those to family members or entities the member is associated with.

- **No Affiliation:** Members must not be 'affiliated persons' of the company or its subsidiaries. Affiliation is determined by control or common control through ownership, contract, or other means.

(b) Safe Harbor Provision

The SEC offers a safe harbor, presuming non-control for anyone not serving as an executive officer or holding 10% of the company's stock. Executive officers, employee-directors, and certain partners or managing members are deemed affiliated.

(c) Exemptions for New Public Companies

SOX provides exemptions for newly public companies, requiring at least one independent audit committee member at the time of going public, a majority within 90 days, and full independence within a year.

(d) Financial Expert Requirement

SOX doesn't mandate a financial expert on the audit committee but requires companies to disclose whether they have one. The SEC enhances this by asking for additional disclosure if not, to encourage having a member with the right qualifications.

(e) Qualifying as a Financial Expert

- An audit committee financial expert, according to the SEC, must have:

- A deep understanding of GAAP and financial statements.

- The ability to assess GAAP in the context of estimates, accruals, and reserves.

- Experience in preparing, auditing, analyzing, or evaluating complex financial statements, or supervising those who do.

- Knowledge of internal control over financial reporting and audit committee functions.

These qualifications can be achieved through various experiences, including roles as financial officers, accountants, auditors, or relevant supervisory positions.

In essence, SOX has set the bar high for audit committee members, ensuring their independence and expertise to uphold the integrity of financial reporting.

5.27 The Audit Committee: Guardians of Auditor Independence

In the realm of corporate governance, the selection and oversight of independent auditors is a pivotal role that ensures the integrity of financial reporting. Here's a breakdown of who's in charge, as per the SOX:

(a) The Audit Committee's Sole Responsibility

SOX mandates that the audit committee, not the

company's management, wields the power to hire, fire, and compensate the independent auditors. This arrangement is critical to maintain the auditor's objectivity. If auditors were to report to management, there could be a conflict of interest, potentially influencing the auditor's willingness to challenge management's financial reporting.

(b) Objective Review Safeguard

To prevent any compromise in the auditor's independence, the audit committee is tasked with overseeing the auditor's work. This includes resolving any discrepancies that may arise between the auditor and management. The committee also has the authority to approve the terms of the audit engagement and any significant non-audit services provided by the auditor.

(c) No Impact on Shareholder Involvement

The SOX rule does not override the requirement for auditors to be elected, approved, or ratified by the company's shareholders. It simply delineates the responsibility allocation of hiring auditors between management and the audit committee. If a company decides to involve shareholders in the decision-making process, it is the audit committee that should make the recommendation to shareholders regarding the election, approval, or ratification of the auditor.

In essence, the audit committee serves as the bulwark against any perceived or actual influence that management could exert over the auditors, thereby safeguarding the auditor's independence and the reliability of the company's financial reporting.

5.28 SOX Whistleblower Provisions: Shielding the Corporate Watchdogs

The SOX is designed to encourage and protect employees who report unethical practices within their companies:

(a) Audit Committee's Role in Safeguarding

SOX mandates that the audit committee establish procedures for receiving, retaining, and addressing complaints about accounting, internal controls, or auditing matters. These procedures must include a secure and anonymous method for employees to report concerns.

(b) Protection Against Retaliation

A key aspect of SOX is the protection it offers to whistleblowers from any form of retaliation, including dismissal, demotion, or harassment, for their role in reporting misconduct.

(c) Enhancing SOX's Integrity Measures

These whistleblower provisions complement and

strengthen other aspects of SOX by providing employees with the confidence to come forward with information about any wrongdoing without fear of repercussions.

In summary, SOX's provisions ensure that employees who expose questionable activities are supported and protected, fostering a corporate environment that prioritizes transparency and accountability.

5.29 Empowerment of the Audit Committee: Hiring Outside Advisors

The audit committee's role in ensuring financial integrity is pivotal, and to fulfill this duty effectively, it may need to seek external expertise. The Securities and Exchange Commission (SEC) recognizes this need and has set guidelines to support the committee's independence and effectiveness:

(a) Unrestricted Access to Resources

The SEC mandates that an audit committee should have the unrestricted authority to hire any outside advisors it deems necessary. This includes legal counsel and other professionals who can provide valuable guidance and advice.

(b) Funding for Independence

To maintain the committee's autonomy, the SEC also requires that the company provide adequate funding as determined by the audit committee. This funding is essential for the committee to operate effectively, hire public accounting firms, or engage other advisors without any financial constraints.

(c) Ensuring Unbiased Oversight

By granting the audit committee the power to engage outside advisors and providing the necessary financial support, the SEC aims to ensure that the committee can perform its oversight role without bias, aligning with the best interests of the company and its shareholders.

In essence, the SEC's rules fortify the audit committee's capacity to uphold its responsibilities with the support it needs, reinforcing the corporate governance framework and bolstering investor confidence.

5.30 SOX Requirements for Disclosure Controls and Financial Reporting

The SOX has set forth specific requirements for companies to ensure the accuracy and reliability of financial reporting:

(a) Disclosure Controls and Procedures

These are mechanisms designed to ensure that all information required by the SEC is properly recorded, processed, and reported. This includes both financial and non-financial information. Companies must periodically evaluate these controls and disclose their effectiveness in quarterly and annual reports.

(b) Internal Control Over Financial Reporting

This involves processes overseen by management to provide assurance on the reliability of financial reporting and the accuracy of financial statements under GAAP. It includes maintaining detailed and timely records of financial transactions.

(c) SOX's Internal Control Report Mandates

SOX requires annual reports to include an internal control report that:

- Acknowledges management's responsibility for establishing and maintaining adequate internal controls for financial reporting.

- Provides an assessment of the effectiveness of these controls at the end of the fiscal year.

(d) Compliance and Evaluation

Public companies must maintain adequate internal controls for financial reporting. Auditors must evaluate and find these controls adequate before rendering an audit opinion. Companies invest significantly in documenting and evaluating these controls to support management's conclusions and the auditor's assessment.

(e) Management's Role

Management should:

- Understand the definition of internal control over financial reporting.

- Organize a team to conduct evaluations.

- Perform evaluations at various levels, from entity to process and transaction specifics.

- Assess overall effectiveness, identify areas for improvement, and establish monitoring systems.

(f) SEC's Expanded Disclosure Rules

These rules require that:

- Management's report on internal controls must be included in the company's annual SEC filing.

- The report must state management's responsibility, the framework used for evaluation, and provide an assessment of control effectiveness, including any material weaknesses.

- The company's auditor must attest to management's

assessment and report on the internal control audit.

(g) Quarterly Reporting Changes

Companies must also disclose any significant changes in internal controls during the period covered by a quarterly report.

In essence, SOX has established a framework that promotes transparency and accountability in financial reporting, with stringent standards for internal controls and management's responsibility to ensure their effectiveness.

5.31 SOX and Non-GAAP Measures: The New Disclosure Paradigm

The SOX prompted the SEC to establish guidelines on the presentation of non-GAAP financial measures, aiming to bring clarity and comparability to financial disclosures:

(a) Regulation G: The Framework

On January 22, 2003, the SEC introduced Regulation G, applying to all public companies and governing the disclosure of non-GAAP financial measures across various public communications, including press releases, investor calls, conference presentations, and annual reports.

(b) Scope and Application

The rules demand that any material non-GAAP financial measures disclosed be accompanied by a clear explanation and a GAAP-compliant equivalent. The stringent requirements for SEC filings contrast with the more lenient approach for oral and webcast presentations.

(c) Exclusions from the Rules

Pro forma disclosures related to proposed business combinations are exempt from these rules, as they are governed by different SEC regulations.

(d) Definition of Non-GAAP Financial Measures

A non-GAAP financial measure is one that omits or includes amounts not present in the most comparable GAAP financial measure. However, certain items are explicitly not classified as non-GAAP measures, such as operational metrics, financial measures mandated by GAAP or SEC rules, and ratios calculated from GAAP-compliant measures.

(e) Examples of Non-GAAP Financial Measures

Examples include operating income measures that exclude "non-recurring" items, EBITDA (which, despite using GAAP elements, does not conform to GAAP presentation), and ratios derived from measures not calculated in accordance with GAAP.

(f) SEC's Informal Stance

The SEC staff has informally indicated that certain financial ratios and measures, such as earnings to fixed charges ratio (as required by SEC rules) and revenues by product line (provided total revenues are also disclosed), are not considered non-GAAP financial measures under the rules.

In essence, SOX, through Regulation G, has set the stage for a more disciplined approach to non-GAAP financial disclosures, ensuring that investors have a transparent and comparable view of a company's financial performance, while allowing companies the flexibility to present additional insights into their operations.

5.32 Presenting Non-GAAP Financial Information: A Guide to Compliance

When public companies wish to present non-GAAP financial information, they must navigate a set of requirements designed to ensure clarity and comparability for investors:

(a) Companions in Disclosure:

Any non-GAAP financial measure must be accompanied by:

- The most directly comparable GAAP financial

measure, and

- A quantitative reconciliation explaining the differences between the non-GAAP and GAAP measures.

(b) SEC's Balancing Act:

While companies have the flexibility to decide what constitutes the "most directly comparable" GAAP measure, the SEC suggests balancing cash flow operations with cash flow statements and performance measures with net income from operations.

(c) Forward-Looking Measures:

If a non-GAAP measure is projected and its GAAP equivalent is not readily available, the company must disclose the unavailable information and its likely significance, providing as much reconciling information as possible.

(d) Clear Reconciliation:

The reconciliation should be presented clearly, either in a schedule format or through another understandable method. For ratios or measures involving non-GAAP components, a reconciliation for each non-GAAP measure and the GAAP equivalent must be provided.

(e) Prominence in SEC Filings:

If the disclosure is part of a document filed with the SEC, the GAAP measure must be at least as prominent as the non-GAAP measure to avoid misleading investors.

(f) Avoiding Misleading Information:

Non-GAAP measures should not obscure GAAP results or be presented before the GAAP measures. The rationale for using non-GAAP measures should be sound, and consistency in their application is key.

(g) Best Practices for Companies:

- Ensure non-GAAP measures do not overshadow GAAP outcomes.

- Present GAAP measures prior to non-GAAP measures in disclosures.

- Have a valid reason for employing non-GAAP measures.

- Maintain consistency in the exclusion or inclusion of items.

- Adhere to the detailed requirements of Item 10(e) of Regulation S-K.

- Disclose any changes in the calculation or presentation of non-GAAP measures and explain the reasons.

- Calculate per share measures on both a diluted and primary basis.
  o

By following these guidelines, companies can provide additional financial insights to investors while maintaining transparency and regulatory compliance.

5.33 Oral Non-GAAP Disclosures: Navigating Regulation G Compliance

When presenting non-GAAP financial information through oral statements, phone calls, webcasts, or similar means, Regulation G offers a pathway for compliance that leverages the company's website:

(a) Website Disclosure Synchronization:

Regulation G allows the required disclosures to be posted on the company's website at the time the non-GAAP information is shared. The audience must be directed to the website for the necessary information.

(b) Application in Various Settings:

This rule applies to contexts such as annual shareholder meetings or conference calls discussing earnings releases.

Planning is essential to ensure disclosures are online in advance of these events.

(c) Exclusion for Supporting Materials:

For slideshows or written handouts that accompany oral presentations, the rule does not apply. These materials must contain the Regulation G disclosures if they include material non-GAAP financial measures.

(d) Caveats to Consider:

If the oral disclosure is about a previous fiscal period not previously disclosed to the public, the press release announcing the event must instruct how to access the Regulation G information on the website. Otherwise, it must be filed on Form 8-K.

Regulation G does not permit compliance through after-the-fact disclosures. The information must be pre-posted or provided immediately during the call.

(e) Inadvertent Disclosures:

Unlike Regulation FD, which has a more lenient approach to unintentional disclosures, Regulation G requires immediate compliance. This is irrespective of compliance with Regulation FD due to prior notice of the call.

(f) Form 8-K Distinction:

Regulation G's requirements differ from the Form 8-K, Item 2.02 provision, which allows up to four business days to disclose material nonpublic information to the SEC, rather than requiring immediate website posting.

In summary, while Regulation G facilitates the oral disclosure of non-GAAP financial information, it necessitates proactive planning and strict adherence to timing and disclosure requirements to ensure compliance.

5.34 Regulation G and Earnings Releases: A Compliance Overview

Regulation G plays a pivotal role in shaping how companies present earnings releases, especially when they include non-GAAP financial measures:

(a) Prominence of GAAP Measures:

Any earnings release filed with the SEC on Form 8-K must present the most directly comparable GAAP financial measure with at least equal prominence as the non-GAAP measure. This rule applies to the original earnings release, meaning that if a non-GAAP measure is headlined, the corresponding GAAP figure must also be highlighted.

(b) Disclosure of Reasons:

If the non-GAAP measure has not been previously disclosed in the most recent Form 10-K, the earnings release must explain why management believes the non-GAAP measure provides useful information to investors, considering the company's business and industry context.

(c) Consistent Application:

Companies that frequently use non-GAAP measures might find it efficient to include the rationale in their Form 10-K to avoid repetition in each release.

(d) Regulation G Requirements:

Non-GAAP measures in SEC filings are subject to strict presentation, reconciliation, explanation, and anti-misleading requirements.

(e) Regulation S-K Item 10(e) Compliance:

This regulation includes several prohibitions and requirements for companies using non-GAAP measures:

- Charges or liabilities that require or will require cash settlement cannot be excluded from non-GAAP liquidity measures. While EBIT and EBITDA are not covered by this rule, they must be properly reconciled to GAAP.

- Non-GAAP performance measures cannot be used to

eliminate items that are likely to recur within two years or have recurred within the prior two years.

- Non-GAAP financial measures must not be presented on the face of GAAP financial statements or in the accompanying notes.

- Non-GAAP measures should not be included in pro forma financial information related to business combinations as required by SEC rules.

- The titles or descriptions of non-GAAP measures must not mimic or be confusingly similar to those used for GAAP measures.

In essence, Regulation G, along with Regulation S-K Item 10(e), ensures that non-GAAP financial measures are presented in a manner that is transparent, comparable, and does not mislead investors, while providing management with the flexibility to share additional financial insights.

5.35 Off-Balance Sheet Financing Disclosure: Unveiling the Invisible

The aftermath of the Enron scandal underscored the importance of transparency in off-balance sheet financing. The SOX responded by pushing for comprehensive disclosure requirements:

(a) SOX-Inspired SEC Rules

SOX mandated the SEC to establish rules that demand companies reveal all material off-balance sheet transactions, arrangements, and obligations in their reports.

(b) Prominent Disclosure Requirement

In any financial statement required document, such as registration statements, annual reports, and proxy statements, companies must include a distinctly-captioned section detailing off-balance sheet arrangements that could materially impact their financial health.

(c) Content of Disclosure

The disclosure should cover:

- The nature and purpose of off-balance sheet arrangements.

- Their significance to the company's liquidity, capital resources, market risk, or credit risk.

- Revenues, expenses, and cash flows derived from these arrangements.

- The company's retained interests, issued securities, and incurred indebtedness related to the arrangements.

- Any obligations or liabilities, including contingent ones, that could become material, along with triggering events.

- Known events or trends that could lead to the termination or reduction of these arrangements and the company's response.

(d) Definition of "Off-Balance Sheet Arrangement"

This term refers to transactions or contractual arrangements with unconsolidated entities involving the company in obligations such as:

- Contingent guarantees and indemnification arrangements.

- Retained or contingent interests in assets transferred to the unconsolidated entity.

- Obligations under contracts that would be considered derivative instruments.

- Obligations arising from a variable interest in an unconsolidated entity providing specific types of support to the company.

(e) Additional Contractual Obligations Disclosure
Companies must also disclose the amount of their known

contractual obligations, categorized by maturity dates, including:

- Long-term debt.

- Capital lease obligations.

- Operating lease obligations.

- Purchase obligations.

- Other long-term liabilities listed on the balance sheet.

In essence, these SOX-prompted rules serve to illuminate the shadows cast by off-balance sheet transactions, ensuring that investors and stakeholders have a clear view of a company's financial commitments and potential risks.

5.36 Audit Influence and Liability: The SEC's Stance

The Securities and Exchange Commission (SEC) has set clear boundaries to prevent improper influence over the auditing process, ensuring the integrity of financial statements:

(a) SEC's Prohibition on Misleading Actions

The SEC has implemented rules that prohibit company officers or directors from engaging in any behavior intended to deceive or mislead accountants. The aim is to prevent financial statements from being rendered materially misleading.

(b) Scope of Prohibited Actions

These rules prohibit any action that could influence, coerce, manipulate, or mislead an accountant in a way that could foreseeably result in misleading financial statements. This includes not only direct actions by directors or officers involved in policy-making but also actions by individuals under their direction, such as customers, vendors, or creditors who provide false or misleading information to auditors at the direction of these officers or directors.

(c) Culpability Criteria

An officer, director, or person acting under their direction is considered culpable if they knowingly engaged in conduct that could result in misleading financial statements. This includes situations where they should have known the potential outcome of their actions.

(d) Duration of Applicability

The rules are applicable throughout the entire professional engagement period of the auditor and extend beyond it when the auditor is deciding whether to consent to the use of the audit report. In some cases, the rules could even apply before the auditor's engagement, such as when a director seeks to hire an accounting firm with the precondition of issuing an unqualified report regardless of GAAP conformity.

(e) Jurisdiction and Enforcement

The SEC holds exclusive jurisdiction to enforce these rules, and there is no provision for private parties to initiate legal action under them.

In summary, the SEC's rules are designed to safeguard the auditing process from undue influence, maintaining the accuracy and reliability of financial reporting and upholding investor confidence in the market.

5.37 Clawback Provisions of SOX: A Safety Net for Financial Integrity

The SOX includes a strong mechanism to hold executives accountable for financial reporting accuracy:

(a) Repayment of Compensation Triggered by Restatement

If a company needs to restate its financial results because of material noncompliance with financial reporting requirements due to misconduct, the CEO and CFO are obligated to repay any bonuses, incentive-based compensation, or profits from the sale of company securities received within a 12-month period following the initial publication of the document that is restated.

(b) The "Clawback" Provision

This repayment requirement is commonly referred to as the "clawback" provision. It serves as a deterrent against misconduct and a means to rectify situations where executives have benefited financially from inaccurate financial reporting.

(c) SEC's Role in Enforcement

The SEC uses the clawback provision to recover profits and bonuses earned by executives that may have misled investors, ensuring that there are consequences for actions that compromise the integrity of financial reporting.

In essence, SOX's clawback provision reinforces the responsibility of executives for the financial statements they present, creating a more transparent and trustworthy business environment.

5.38 SOX's Broad Reach: Implications for Directors and Officers

Beyond the well-known provisions, the SOX extends its influence over directors and officers in several significant ways:

(a) Lowered Unfitness Standard

SOX has revised the criteria for determining unfitness to serve as an officer or director of a public company. The SEC now has the authority to issue cease-and-desist orders against individuals who have violated specific sections of the Securities Exchange Act or the Securities Act, demonstrating unfitness through their conduct. This shift simplifies the process of barring individuals from serving in public companies.

(b) Protection for Whistleblowers

Two distinct provisions in SOX safeguard individuals who aid in investigations:

- It's criminalized to take retaliatory actions against anyone providing truthful information on potential federal offenses to law enforcement.

- Public companies and their affiliates are prohibited from discriminating against employees who offer information or assist in investigations related to alleged SEC rule violations or federal securities fraud.

(c) Legal Redress for Retaliation

Employees who face adverse actions due to their participation in investigations have access to civil damages, including attorney's fees, as a form of recourse.

(d) Additional Key Provisions

Other notable aspects of SOX include:

- CEO and CFO must certify the accuracy of SEC filings.

- It's a criminal offense to tamper with or conceal documents to hinder investigations or bankruptcy proceedings.

- The SEC has the power to suspend payments to executives during investigations.

- Enhanced penalties for fraud and securities violations are made non-dischargeable in bankruptcy.

- The SEC must establish a rule for the timely reporting of all material events.

In essence, SOX reinforces corporate accountability and transparency, with provisions that impact the responsibilities and potential liabilities of directors and officers, while also providing protections for those who contribute to the detection and prevention of fraud and misconduct.

5.39 Dodd-Frank Act: A Sea Change in Financial Regulation

The Dodd-Frank Wall Street Reform and Consumer Protection Act, enacted in 2010, was a monumental response to the financial crisis, aiming to reshape the financial industry and corporate accountability:

(a) Say-on-Pay

This provision mandates public companies to hold a non-binding shareholder vote to approve executive compensation. Shareholders can decide on the frequency of these votes, choosing between annual, biennial, or triennial say-on-pay votes, with an initial choice every six years.

(b) Golden Parachute Compensation

The Act introduces requirements for the disclosure and shareholder approval of golden parachute arrangements for named executive officers in the context of mergers, acquisitions, or significant asset sales. Shareholders must approve these arrangements unless they have been previously subject to a say-on-pay vote.

(c) Compensation Committee Independence

All U.S. listed companies are required to have fully independent compensation committees. These committees are tasked with selecting consultants, legal counsel, and advisors, considering SEC-defined independence factors. Proxy statements must detail the committee's relationships with consultants and any conflicts of interest.

(d) Executive Pay Versus Performance

The Dodd-Frank Act instructs the SEC to amend rules for proxy statement disclosures to illustrate the link between executive compensation and company financial performance. While rules were proposed, they had not been finalized at the time of the Act's discussion.

(e) Pay Ratio Disclosures

The Act mandates the SEC to enforce rules that require companies to disclose the ratio of the CEO's compensation to the median compensation of all employees. Exemptions apply to certain types of companies, and non-U.S. employees can be excluded under certain conditions.

(f) Clawback Policies

Publicly listed companies must develop and disclose clawback policies that enable the recovery of incentive-based compensation from executives if the company restates its financials due to material noncompliance. The SEC was working on related rules but had not finalized them at the time.

(g) Employee/Director Hedging

The Act requires companies to disclose in their annual proxy statements whether employees or directors are allowed to hedge or offset the market value decrease of their equity securities. Proposed rules were issued by the SEC, but they were not finalized at the time.

In essence, the Dodd-Frank Act has significantly impacted executive compensation, corporate governance, and transparency, with the aim of preventing future financial crises and protecting investors.

Appendix A: Sample Timetable for an IPO and Listing of Common Stocks on NASDAQ or NYSE

Time	Descriptions
Week 1	• Organizational meeting • Begin legal review • Begin Due Diligence
Week 1 - 2	• Commence preparation of Registration Statement and Underwriting Agreement
Week 3	• Circulate drafts of Registration Statement and Underwriting Agreement • Meetings to discuss drafts of Registration Statement and Underwriting Agreement
Week 4	• Draft of Registration Statement to printer • Circulate proofs of Registration Statement and Underwriting Agreement • Meeting to discuss Registration Statement
Week 5 - 6	• Meetings to discuss revised proofs of Registration Statement

Capitalizing on Dreams: Guide to U.S. IPO & Listings

Time	Descriptions
Week 6	• Meeting of Board of Directors to approve filing of Registration Statement and other matters in connection with offering • File FINRA materials
Week 7	• Meeting to finalize Registration Statement • Listing Application filed with NYSE/NASDAQ • Registration Statement filed with SEC
Week 11	• Receive comments from SEC • Meeting of all parties to discuss SEC comments (if necessary) • File amendment to Registration Statement with SEC
Week 12	• Commence "roadshow" marketing efforts
Week 12 - 13	• Receive additional comments from the SEC and finalize Registration Statement
Week 14	• Registration Statement becomes effective; determine offering price of stock and underwriting discounts; sign Underwriting Agreement; commence sale of stock
Pricing + 3 Business Days	• Closing

Capitalizing on Dreams: Guide to U.S. IPO & Listings

WhatsApp　　　**WeChat**　　　**IPO DreamWorks**

Capitalizing on Dreams: Guide to U.S. IPO & Listings

For Cooperation, Consultation or Join Group, Please Contact (Tel / WhatsApp / WeChat): +1 (917) 985 7989 (U.S.); +852 5162 6310 (HK); +86 152 1081 6303 (China); Email: CEO@USFinance.Org. If You Also Wish to Publish Your Book(s) Globally, Please Contact Us or Send Us Manuscript(s).

WhatsApp   WeChat   IPO DreamWorks

www.ingramcontent.com/pod-product-compliance
Lightning Source LLC
Chambersburg PA
CBHW071450220526
45472CB00003B/754